Find Your Own

Happiness

Mary K. Mills

Julie,
  May you always have your
dreams fulfilled.

                    May K. Mills

BLACK ❦ ROSE
writing™

First printing

The author has tried to recreate events, locales and conversations from her memories. In order to maintain anonymity in some instances, the author may have changed the names of individuals and places. The author may have changed some identifying characteristics and details such as physical properties, occupations and places of residence.

ISBN: 978-1-61296-503-1

PUBLISHED BY BLACK ROSE WRITING

www.blackrosewriting.com

Printed in the United States of America

Suggested retail price $15.95

Find Your Own Happiness is printed in Gentium Book Basic

Author Photograph courtesy of Todd McGinnis

Cover Painting courtesy of Jay Davis

This book is dedicated to all my family and friends. You have all enriched my life in more ways than I can say. Thank you.

Acknowledgments

A special thank you to Andrea Price, writer and editor extraordinaire and owner of Compass Writing, who inadvertently gave me the title of this book one day in the Grand Canyon, when I needed a lift the most. Without her help, this book could not have been written.

Thank you to Peggy Mitchell who helped me with editing.

A heartfelt thank you to my siblings Dianne, Karen, Leslie, and Johnny. I can't imagine a life as an only child. With you I have weathered every storm and had a life full of love, laughter, and worth living. Thank you for all your support through the years. This book would not have been possible without having such awesome siblings that believed in me. Even though Dianne and Karen are no longer with us, their love for me will always keep me strong.

To my parents, Dick and Anne Leatherbury, who are missed every day. You never let me say I couldn't do anything and believed in me in all my endeavors. You encouraged me to be the first person in our family to go to college and instilled in me a love of literature and writing. Thank you for your unconditional love and unwavering support.

You are given your family and I am lucky to have the best, but you choose your friends and they pick you. My friends never let me say "no" or "I can't" and always push me to strive to be the best I can be. They have been there through laughter, tears, and calls in the middle of the night. Thank you to all my friends too numerous to mention and whose support led me to believe that I can move mountains. You know who you are and I hope you know how much you mean to me and how much your support and encouragement helped me write this book. Your friendship means the world to me. Lastly a special thanks to my students that I have taught over the last 25 years; you were as diverse as the stars in the sky. I learned something from all of you and you left your mark on my heart. I always told you that you should follow your dreams and you told me the same, so I wrote this book.

Find Your Own

Happiness

Introduction

This book is my story, a story of hope and happiness. A story that could have had a very different ending if I hadn't made the choice to be happy and do whatever it took to overcome tremendous grief and adversity to achieve this goal, to find my own happiness. It was not always an easy journey. Sometimes I felt I had succeeded only to be dealt another devastating blow. I managed to be happy most of the time in spite of life conspiring against me. I made the conscious decision that I would not fall into depression and despair and that I would take whatever steps were necessary to live a wonderful life in honor of my loved ones who weren't with me any longer.

This story covers two distinctive stories in my life. One is the story of growth and self-discovery that I had intended the book to be, then I did something that so profoundly changed me and tied all the missing pieces together I couldn't have left it out. I kayaked 280 miles of the Colorado River through the Grand Canyon. That trip summed up everything I had felt, experienced, and been striving for, so I went back and wove the Grand Canyon Trip into my life story. Those chapters are listed by the days spent on the river and alternate with the rest of my life. As you read about my Grand Canyon trip and go back to experience my life, you can see the connection. Both rivers, the river of events that shaped me, and the mighty Colorado River that showed me sometimes you just have to go with the flow and accept where the river tosses you. Two journeys, one over a lifetime and one over 12 days.

Table of Contents

Chapter 1

Change

So what if you woke up one morning and your entire world changed? The rest of the world was moving as if nothing happened, and yet, here you are feeling like you are alone on a sea of change drowning in the terrifying newness that has become the reality of your life. So what sparked this change? Ten days earlier my husband was diagnosed with stage four lung cancer, and now just a little more than a week later I sat alone, a widow, in my huge house wondering what I was going to do.

This story actually starts 18 years earlier, when I was 19, young, and full of ideas and dreams. I had been on my own for a year living in the dorms in college and was enjoying exploring new things and finding myself. I was the first person in my family to go to college and I was enjoying my second year there. I've always had my father's adventurous spirit so I took up Scuba Diving. I had never done anything very athletic in my life and since I loved the water, this was ideal. I took some classes and started going on group trips. I first met Jim on a Scuba Diving trip in Ft. Lauderdale. I remember him standing on the dock, looking cocky and confident, leaning up against the dock smoking a cigarette. We were drift diving, which is where you float with the current pulling along a flag on a buoy attached to a long rope. I was having trouble managing this and Jim swam over and took the rope from me and stayed with my group during the dives. Shortly after, he moved to St. Petersburg where I was living at the time and started working in a Scuba Shop. I started working there as well. We went on many dive trips together and started spending more and more time together. I fell in love with him even though he was 25 years my senior. I know what you are thinking, and now looking back I feel the same thing. But sometimes, love supersedes common sense. I also feel, now that I have had time to reflect, that I have the type personality where I like to care for others and make them happy, which added to the intrigue I initially felt toward Jim that I thought was love. In reality I was infatuated and thought that I could make him happy and take care of him. I knew he had never really been happy in his life and I felt that he really needed me. And for once in his life, he could find happiness and love with me.

My parents amazingly accepted Jim and he became part of my family. He had no family of his own. We were married just two years later when I was 21. I had graduated from college around then with a degree in special education and was looking forward to beginning a career teaching. From the beginning, our marriage was an odd one due to the age difference. There were days when all was well and it seemed that life couldn't get any better. We bought a small home in an area in Tampa, Florida that we loved and settled in. Jim felt the need to make me happy with things and gifts. I missed having a pet and he helped me adopt my first cat. We went to the Humane Society and in the bottom cage was this scrawny, sickly yellow tabby that looked at me with the most pitiful eyes. We adopted her and named her Cuddles and I loved her. When we first started dating, he was very attentive, happy, and easy going. I rarely heard him yell or lose his temper. I knew he had found in me the love he had never had in his life. He was never close to his family, had failed marriages, and had always been lost in life. The feelings he had for me were genuine. I enjoyed having someone love me so completely.

I am not sure when things started to change, but slowly I noticed he would get upset more frequently and we would have fights over trivial and unimportant issues. I could never express an opposing viewpoint or tell my side of the story without invoking more anger or irritation so I just said I was sorry and let it go. He was always right in any argument and any arguing with him did no good. Rather it made me cry and made him yell longer. The frequency of the disagreements increased over time and also started occurring over more trivial things. Sometimes it was the way I washed clothes. He insisted that blue shirts had to be on blue hangers and clothes folded a certain way. After many heated arguments that left me in tears, he finally agreed to do the laundry because I could never do it correctly. But I felt inadequate. I should have been able to figure out the system to please him. There were many more signs, that were small things, but put together were not so small. Spices had to be alphabetized and the pen/junk drawer in the kitchen had to be very organized. If these things weren't done in the particular and precise fashion, he would get irritated. As the years went on, his irritation turned to anger and my frustration grew. I couldn't figure out why I could not do things right to make him happy. I remember always having a fear in the pit of my stomach, a constant worry that I would do something wrong and set him off and more deeply why I couldn't do things right enough.

I know what you are thinking. I should have seen the signs. I should have realized there was something controlling about him. After all I am intelligent, a professional, a teacher, why didn't I see it? Maybe I did, but like many women, I was sure if I did everything right he would be happy. I could fix him. He hadn't been this way while we were dating and wasn't always so controlling or picky, but the times were getting more and more frequent. I organized the spices by ABC order, I kept the drawers neat, and we ate what he wanted to eat. Many days life was good, and I felt we had a normal marriage. Amazingly enough, looking back on those early marriage years I feel like we were happy most of the time. We had annual passes to Disney World and frequented the parks. I remember one Florida state park in particular where we would bring hamburgers and have cookouts under the shelter and feed the squirrels as they begged for food. One we were there, and a rain storm came up and we spent hours under the shelter playing cards and laughing about things.

Throughout the entire marriage I never felt like I was in an abusive relationship. I always felt I was in a normal marriage. But I could detect a tension that was starting to develop, a nagging feeling that I might do something wrong. I had constant butterflies in the pit of my stomach, apprehensive that I would say something to make him angry. I was being too careful what I said, and I, a normally extremely talkative person became quiet, not offering my opinions. One thing that really would make him incredibly angry is if I fell asleep in the car while he was driving. I never figured out why this upset him so much but it would spark almost fury on his part. I have always been able to fall asleep quickly and cars put me to sleep. Jim wasn't a music fan and preferred talk radio stations and I was afraid to talk most times, so I would often drift off. This would just spark rage and unending yelling and belittling me.

I am a messy person by nature, so keeping things as neat as he wanted was not easy for me. I'm not dirty, but I have always felt a little clutter isn't a bad thing. My poor organizational skills, messiness, and the inability to do things his way became the point of almost a daily fight which resulted in my crying and promising to do things better. But still I felt at the time the good times in our marriage outweighed the bad. Now I realize that a subtle change in my personality was occurring. I was careful to do things that wouldn't upset him. I was quiet most of the time, easier to be quiet than to risk saying the wrong thing. I had a constant little worry in the pit of my stomach that I would do something wrong to upset him. I was living in fear, but it was such a part of my daily life I hadn't even noticed. I got out of work as quickly as I could get home to him; otherwise he would accuse me of not wanting to spend time with him or occasionally of having an affair with someone. I had to call him when I got to work and when I left. This was not an option. My parents had had an ideal marriage so I had a good role models, but still I didn't see that there was anything wrong with our marriage. I just assumed that everyone's marriage was this way.

Now my husband didn't fit into the normal mold of a controller as far as I can tell. He actually had a kind side. Any stray animal was picked up and taken care of. If he heard about a student of mine doing without he made sure he/she had what was needed to be happy and successful in school whether it was clothing or food. So once again I felt for sure if I just did everything right, he wouldn't be so angry and would be happy. How could a person that cared about animals, children, and other people be so bad? He said he loved me and showed me in many ways. But underneath it all, I still had the constant nagging fear that I would do something wrong that would spark his anger and my tears. I was convinced it was my fault and not his. Since I was the one irritating him, it must have been my fault, right?

I try to explain this to people and I see their look of "How could you stay there?" I just don't know the answer. It happened so gradually and subtly, that I hardly know when the abuse began or maybe it had always been in the relationship, but worsened as time went on. This never happened while we were dating. After we were married, things didn't change overnight. The fights and anger came on gradually. First I had to always stay in contact with him and he had to know my location at every second and preferably be with me if he could. He isolated me from my friends and for the entire marriage there was no one I could call a close friend. I had friends at work I talked to and liked, but I tried to keep my distance for fear one of them would ask me to go somewhere and I would not be able to. The only time I was alone was driving to and from work and during the workday. Even in the house we were always in the same room and I never, ever shut a door, not even the bathroom when I was in it.

Eventually I just called him when I got to work each day and when I left to appease him so he didn't get angry with me. I didn't see it as controlling, but rather that he loved me and was worried about me. After all on weekends we did fun things together. We went on walks, watched TV, played video games, read. Life was pretty good as long as I did things right and followed his directions. He told me he loved me constantly and felt this overwhelming fear that he was going to lose me. He would often get me candy, chocolate, or other gifts, most likely for his guilt at treating me so badly. He would leave me notes around the house and never forgot my birthday or major holidays.

In your twenties, most people haven't formed their identity yet. During these years I was with Jim, and I now realize he was defining who I was becoming. My political, environmental, social, and moral issues were forming and most of them were forming on his opinions and beliefs. According to him, his opinions were facts and if I, or anyone else, disagreed with him he called me stupid and other names until I was sure my opinions were wrong and his were right. There was no opposing viewpoint as far as he was concerned. I never disagreed with him for fear of sparking a fight, which were always long drawn out affairs that left him in a very bad mood and me in tears, begging him to forgive me. So what I thought were my beliefs on things were really in fact his and based on his beliefs and viewpoints.

In the beginning it was yelling for some minor infraction. As the years progressed, it was name calling, ugly, stupid, fat, and saying constantly that I could do nothing right and no one would ever want to be around me. When you are told these things daily, you believe them. I was beginning to feel inadequate and had an overwhelming fear that no one really wanted me around. I was constantly worried I would say something wrong, stupid, or irritating. There were times I thought of leaving him, but the threats were extreme. He would file for alimony, he would take the cats and all our belongings. He would take everything I had and make sure I could not live. He would ruin me. I was also afraid of the unbelievable anger I'm sure my leaving would provoke. He rarely had a job and I was pretty much supporting him so I was sure he would win and get some kind of alimony that would make it impossible for me to live on a teacher's salary.

Another source of grief was that he was also extremely jealous of other men. It was especially bad for me if I had to work with men on my team or on the same grade level at school. If I mentioned them at all in any conversation, he accused me of cheating or liking them. If I didn't mention them, he thought I was hiding something. I could never win that argument. It was a lose/lose situation. Even if some male in a store said something and I was friendly back, it could lead to the accusations and fights. I grew up in a very supportive family with the ideal parent and family structure. But my self-esteem and self-worth were being whittled down. After a while you begin to believe the things that are said about you. I am not sure how it happens. Maybe because it is reinforced every day and happens so gradually, you don't notice the change in your perceptions of yourself. I still struggle with self-esteem and image issues as well as weight. I was told I was fat for so long I believe it and have trouble losing weight, a self-fulfilling image I'm assuming that I've never been able to shake off.

When people think of abuse, they normally think of physical, hitting, etc. Jim never once laid a hand on me. It took me many years after his death to admit how abusive he really was. Even as I write this, I find it difficult to put it on paper, hard to accept it as fact. I was in denial as to the abusive nature of our relationship. I remember the first time it really hit me how controlling and abusive he was. I was on a kayaking trip in Costa Rica about a year and a half after Jim died. The trip was led by Juliet and Ken, a couple who owned Endless River Adventures Outfitters, and they had separate groups, so our paths crossed occasionally. I was amazed that they didn't have to be in constant contact with one another. I started noticing this in other couples. I was just stunned. How could they be in different rooms, have different interests, and do things separately without starting a fight or argument? I had never realized marriage could be like that, totally secure with each other and not living in constant fear. It was such an emotional hit that it felt almost physical. How could I not have seen how controlling and abusive Jim was? What was ironic about that really is that my parents had an ideal relationship and never said unkind words to each other. I had the absolute perfect role models for a successful, healthy marriage. Clearly I had been putting the blame for things going wrong on myself, and it hit me hard that day and made me start reflecting on things. Sometimes you just need a kick in the psyche and something that should have been obvious, now becomes perfectly clear to you and opens up your mind so you are able to see clearly and heal. From that point on, I viewed my marriage differently and it opened a door for me, a door to the truth and what the marriage was really like.

My husband never did anything halfway. He was obsessed about things being perfect and orderly. Our lawn and yard was another source of endless unhappiness and fights. We had to have the perfect Saint Augustine grass lawn. So we mowed, watered, bagged our clippings, edged, etc. It took hours in the Florida sun. At least once a week out we went and it was like torture to me and I hated every minute of it. We had to weed by hand to make sure nothing crept into his perfect lawn. The other thing he was obsessed with were roses. By my last count there were close to 100 of them in our yard. Roses are not an easy maintenance plant. I had to constantly prune them, week the beds, water them and spray them for fungus and insects. I'd come home from teaching so tired and yet I had to go out to the lawn and work on these roses for hours. We'd cut the roses and bring them into the house, which was the only good thing about that whole rose incident. To this day I despise working in the lawn or garden. It brings back too many bad memories, and roses to me symbolize a sad chapter in my life. I hope one day to be able to enjoy roses as much as I enjoy other flowers.

By July of 2005 we had moved to Georgia. I had lived in Florida my entire life and wanted a change. He had always hated living in Florida and was happy to make the move. I thought moving to an area he liked better and a move in general might improve things and our marriage. My husband didn't work at this time due to drawing Social Security and retirement, but I had always been the primary breadwinner. I took a job teaching middle school in Georgia. I felt this might be a positive move when my first interaction with someone from my new school was Debbie Garner. She called me up and welcomed me to the school, telling me to come to work the first day like we were going to the beach for team pictures. Her enthusiasm was evident even over the phone. She made me feel welcome into team 7A and has been a friend to me ever since.

My husband stayed home while I worked and I had hoped he would do most of the cleaning and yard work, but that wasn't the case. Just like in Florida I would come home and have to work in the lawn and around the house. My life was almost entirely under his control by this point, although I didn't realize it at the time. He made all the decisions regarding what we ate, what we did, what we watched on TV and every other detail of our life. I always stayed in the same room with him and we went to bed at the same time. I realized that I had no friends outside of him and I hadn't driven anywhere alone except to work in years. He ran my entire life and wouldn't let me socialize with anyone outside of work. He had convinced me that in a marriage the spouses were always together and if I wanted to go out with friends, it meant I didn't love him. Once again, I am unsure how to answer your questions of how I lived like that and why I stayed. Perhaps people who have been in similar relationships can relate, but even I have trouble understanding why I put up with it and lived that way. To this day, I don't think he was an awful man. He had a good side with his caring ways toward stray animals and children. We had fun together on many occasions and there was much laughter in our lives. But after years of looking back and being honest, the anger and fear in my life were much more prevalent. I'm not sure how I convinced myself we had a good and healthy marriage.

I am not sure what caused the anger and controlling issues that he had over me. He once told me he was just so afraid of losing me he couldn't stand it. I guess this might have been brought on from his unhappy family life. He felt that he had never been part of a loving family. We had the never-ending arguments about cleanliness and orderliness, as well as him making most decisions. I can hardly remember a day without tears, anxiety, or fear of making him upset, which of course was always my fault. The verbal abuse and constant unhappiness were escalating to the point that I was literally afraid to talk at all. So I stopped talking, which ironically also irritated him. Then I would try to talk and he would yell at me for saying the wrong thing. I voted for whom he said to vote for, terrified he would find out I voted for another candidate. He always listened to conservative talk radio stations when we were in the car and would still not allow music. I missed music in my life. I really don't think Jim thought of himself as abusive and I'm guessing most abusers don't. He always thought we had a loving healthy relationship.

By February of 2006, school was out for a week for winter break. My husband has always been in good shape and we often went to Georgia state parks to go for short hikes. While at Moccasin State Park, after walking for a mile I noticed he was out of breath and asked to sit on a bench. He reached over and held my hand and looked at me quite lovingly. Did he know something was wrong deep inside? He had a loving and sweet look on his face, very tenderly holding my hand as we looked at the beautiful scenery. We sat there for a while and then turned and went back to the car. He never let me drive and he drove home even though I could tell he wasn't well. I noticed his light cough and heavy breathing on the way home.

The next week I went back to work and Jim was still not feeling well. His cough persisted and his back was in constant pain. So reluctantly he went to a doctor, which is not easy for a man to do. The first doctor told him he had GERD, so he took heartburn medicine and still the symptoms persisted. Back to a specialist when his cough and pain worsened, this doctor said it was allergies, so he started allergy medicines. Still his cough persisted and his back pain was excruciating. One new doctor told him that too many jumps out of airplanes in his youth had resulted in a degenerative disc in his spine. So he started a battery of medications to combat the persistent cough and back pain. As we moved through March, the pain in his back intensified dramatically. The medication did not help his cough, which now resembled an asthma type wheeze. The doctors still insisted that it was GERD and allergies. An orthopedist recommended an MRI on his spine since the pain was almost unbearable. Results came back negative other than some degeneration in a disc. Sometimes you just know something is wrong regardless of what the doctors tell you. It was obvious to me that something was seriously wrong and the doctors were just missing it. I felt helpless and unsure what more we could do.

So he got injections in his spine to try to alleviate the pain, which had worsened to the point he could barely walk. Still bothered by the cough and shortness of breath, he stayed in a chair all day while I taught, unable to get out of it in most cases due to excruciating back pain. At one point I bought him a urinal so he would not have to get up to walk to the restroom when I wasn't there, I was worried he would fall and not be able to get up alone. March 23rd was a Friday and it had been a long week of worrying about him. I knew we only had one more week to go before spring break. I was hoping to find someone to find the answers and make him well. The pain had taken a lot of the fighting out of our marriage. He was so consumed just trying to get by that we hadn't had an argument or any yelling episodes in weeks. By 6:00pm the pain was so bad we took him to the emergency room. He was a tough guy and I had never seen him in this much pain, even after having heart surgery. They couldn't find anything wrong and they gave him some morphine and sent us home. Saturday, March 24th, was one of the longest days I have ever experienced in my life. Jim could barely breathe and I had given him my asthma inhaler to help his breathing. He was now unable to get out of bed at all and could barely move. I kept trying to get him to go back to the hospital, but he was stubborn.

We went to bed around 9:00, thirty minutes later I was awakened to his retching noises. I grabbed the trash can and held it up for him just in time for him to start heaving up blood from his lungs. He just couldn't stop and streams of dense blood just poured out of him into the can. I was terrified. I was going to call 911, but he wouldn't let me and insisted that I drive him to the hospital. It took me over an hour to get him down two flights of stairs and into the car in the garage. It was agonizing for both of us. There was nothing I could do and the minutes crept by like hours to get him down the stairs and to the hospital, which thankfully was a short drive from our house.

I felt a tremendous sense of relief mixed with fear as we pulled up to the hospital. I felt like finally we were going to get some help and answers. I know this sounds crazy, but we both thought maybe he just had pneumonia from sitting and lying down so much. We had been seeing doctors and specialists right along. They had all insisted it was nothing serious. The hospital took chest X-Rays that showed fluid in the lungs. The rural hospital did not have a pulmonary specialist so he would have to be transferred to the larger branch of the hospital in Atlanta. An ambulance was arranged for transportation. After talking with Jim, he wanted me to go home and come back in the morning in Atlanta instead of my driving there in the dark. I hesitantly said good-bye and went home. This was the first time in my adult life that I slept in a home alone. I was 38. One thing Jim always did was control every little thing I ate. This was not so much from a diet standpoint because I was still very overweight then, but just a control thing. I left the hospital and got enough fast food for two people and went home and virtually inhaled it. It was like a sweet rebellion and I knew he wouldn't catch me since I planned to take the trash out with me. That night of the fast food started a food addiction trend with me that I am still struggling to break to this day. I left the lights on and barely slept though that agonizingly slow night. I waited for the first rays of the sun so I could head to Atlanta.

I was in Atlanta by 8:00am. The doctor, Dr. K., was very nice and helpful. They were running tests and should know more soon. Jim was finally fairly pain free now due to pain medication and he was breathing better. They had installed a drainage tube into his lungs and I could see the reddish liquid emptying from his lungs into the container by the bed. We spent the weekend in the hospital hoping for answers. Jim insisted I go to work on Monday. When I arrived at the hospital on March 27th after work, I had no idea how quickly my life was going to change. Dr. K. came in, looked at us both and in the most compassionate way possible told us he had stage 4 lung cancer and it has spread everywhere. The pain in his back was caused by tumors on his spine. He had no clue why the previous MRI had missed.

We listened quietly and in shock as he told us the options, none of which were good. My husband had quit smoking 15 years before so they had not first suspected lung cancer. No one had ever thought to order a chest x ray. The best case scenario was a six-month prognosis. He had blood in his lungs and until the bleeding stopped he could not go home since they won't discharge someone with drainage tubes. I am sure the doctor went into more details, but it was one of those times when everything was in a haze and I couldn't focus on his words. A fog had descended on me and I could not make sense of what he was saying. Experimental drugs, radiation, chemo, pain management. These words hopped out and stuck, but not much else did. In a crazy state of mind I kept thinking of Lance Armstrong. He beat it. They told him his chances were low, maybe Jim could beat the odds too. I remember the doctor walking out of the room and the silence that fall over us, heavy and oppressive. What could I say?

Jim was very practical. They could do what they could do, but no heroic measures, no more pain. He just wanted to get home, pet our cats, and die there. The next eight days were a blur. Every day the doctor told us of a different body part that the cancer had spread to. Brain, kidney, blood, it was everywhere. He had blood transfusions and as I silently said a prayer of thanks to the people whose blood allowed my husband some more days in this world. I wondered if they would be upset it was being used on someone who really had no hope. We endured radiation treatments on his brain every day. I helped place him on the table and comfort him before and after the procedure. The bleeding from his lungs would not stop. Then they tried a procedure where some kind of powder was placed in his lungs and I had to turn him over every 15 minutes to get it to stick to stop the bleeding. Breathing treatments, medication, morphine pumps, and still the bleeding continued. I was desperate to do what he wanted and get him home to die. Dr. K was one of the most compassionate doctors I have ever encountered and the nurses were exceptional. They tried to make my miserable experience more bearable. But if his bleeding from his lungs were not controlled, he could not be discharged.

I could tell my husband had had enough. He just wanted to go home. We talked more and more about his death and what that would mean to us. I think Jim might have had some inkling of how hard this would be on me. He had to have known how in control of my life he had been. My anxiety was increasing daily. I was on my own for the first time in my life at the age of 38 dealing with a terminally ill husband. I hadn't driven more than a few miles in years and I was commuting to and from Atlanta daily in the dark.

On April 5th he asked me to take his will to the lawyer to make sure it was OK. I did that and showed up at the hospital around noon. He looked awful and his breathing was labored. The doctor came in and took me in the hallway. Jim had made a decision. There was no way to stop the bleeding. His pain was being controlled with morphine, but there was no hope of any further treatment and he could not go home with drainage tubes. Jim, in a last gift to me, had signed papers refusing all treatment but pain management. DNR (Do Not Resuscitate Orders) had been signed. He would have no needles, procedures, or anything else done to him other than pain management. I would not have to face the decision of removing support, what kind of care to give, or medical decisions since he was of sound mind and signed the orders to withdrawal everything, but pain medication. Now it was a cruel waiting game.

My father had died in almost the same manner six years before, so I had not told my mother or family the entire truth. Holding the hand of a loved one that dies from anything is awful, but lung cancer is especially painful to bear and I wanted to spare them that, especially my mother. I had of course told her and my siblings that he had lung cancer but had not told them how advanced or close to the end he was. I picked up the phone and called my mother. She was coming with my sister, Leslie, and my brother, John.

The previous school year I had taught a student named Jordan. His dad had passed away that year and his mom, Sherry, worked in our office. I could think of no one else to call. I called her in tears and told her everything. I told her my husband's wishes and she went to work. We were not church people, so I am still unclear why Jim wanted a service with just the two of us and an Episcopal Priest, not an easy thing to find in rural Georgia. He wanted no funeral, cremation, no fuss. Sherry assured me she would have everything settled for me and pick me up when I needed it. It took a lot for me to reach out to someone for help like that and I'm extremely grateful to Sherry for my first experience with friendship in quite some time.

I am not sure now what memories are real, fabricated, or a mix thereof during the next 24 hours. Jim could talk at first, but barely, more of a labored whisper. The tube was removed from his lungs. I'd like to believe he wasn't in pain due to the morphine pump, which I pushed for him frequently. We chatted for a while, mostly words, a phrase here and there in a morphine and lack of oxygen stupor. He was hoping to see the TV show "Lost" that night, a favorite of ours, although I doubt he could comprehend anything. We were watching the show and I was holding his hand when he started convulsing. I buzzed for the night nurse, Scott, who quickly showed up. There was nothing he could do, but hold my hand, as I watched horrified and wishing beyond all hopes he was beyond

24

knowing what was going on and pain free. I, of course, had no such luck. I was acutely aware of what was happening. I would not wish watching a loved one die on my very worst enemy. The overall helplessness you feel just holding his hand, watching him slide away, having a seizure in this case, then just stop moving.

Jim never moved again. From 10:00 that night on, I sat by his bed and held his hand, swabbed his lips, wiped his brow. His eyes were fixed open, unblinking and he was breathing like Darth Vader. The nurse and I changed his sheets because the doctor had promised my husband no procedures and he would not even allow a catheter put in. His skin was blue or yellow and honestly, if I had just walked in, I would not have recognized him. I am sure he was past knowing anything at this point, but I wasn't. When dealing with this kind of grief mixed with lack of sleep, your senses are hyper acute. I felt everything with an intensity I wished would turn to numbness. Scott, the night nurse, often came in when he could and sat with me to comfort me. I will be forever grateful for his kindness and compassion in one of the most difficult times of my life. His compassion and caring were well beyond what was expected. He was a bright spot in a very dark time.

I sat there till 8:00 am the next morning when Dr. K came in between surgeries and insisted I let a clergy member come in. I was numb and I barely heard him. I still can't remember who the clergy was or even if it was male or female. I remember a presence with us in the room, someone talking, but my mind was hyper focused on Jim. I absorbed everything about him in those last moments. It was evident with his lack of movement and ragged breathing that the end was close. The most agonizing moments you will ever spend is holding the hand of a dying loved one, hoping the end comes quickly to end the suffering of both of you, then feeling guilty because you want it to end. How can you be praying hard hoping so strongly for the death of a loved one? An odd thought crossed my head at this time. I would never ever let a pet of mine suffer like this because it would be considered animal cruelty. How we can let our loved ones suffer like this just escapes me.

At about 10:00 AM, Jim shuddered and gave a ragged breath, once more, and he passed. Just like that. No peaceful look. He just stopped making that awful breathing sound, his chest stopped moving, and the room was eerily quiet. His skin fluctuated between yellowish and purplish, his eyes and lips were frozen open and he barely looked human. I honestly would never have recognized him as the man I had been married to for fourteen years. I knew he had passed and was sure of it even before the doctor came in to confirm. Death has its own look. I was dumbfounded, exhausted, and unable to think, move, or make any kind of decision. I could barely remember how to use the phone to call Sherry. I am not sure how long I sat there alone with the body, not sure what I would do next. Lost, alone, terrified, sad. How could I function alone? The nurses had tried to get me to move to another room, but I couldn't move. It hit me so suddenly that I had no one to tell me what to do. I was terrified and mixed with an overwhelming sense of loss, grief, and uncertainty. There is no way words on this paper can convey to you the fear I had at that moment. I have never been so panicked and grief stricken in my entire life. I was in shock for sure, but more than that I just could not imagine living my life under my own means without Jim's constant directions. Finally a knock and Sherry had come with her sister to drive me home, an hour away. I have no memory of the drive except Sherry's calm words, reassuring and having everything under control. She had arranged everything from funeral, priest, transportation, everything. I just sat there crying in the passenger seat. Lost.

I will never forget the abject loneliness I felt when Sherry drove away and left me alone in that house. I felt like I had been tossed alone in the world with no direction. My cats could sense I was unhappy and I just sat there with a cat on my lap, crying. I had never done anything in 15 years without his knowledge or approval. I had rarely even been alone in a room in the house. Julie, from school, had come and taken care of the house, mowed, the lawn, cleaned up. Glenn and Sue along with Debbie completed our team and the four of them got me through those first days. I was thankful for my friends from work. I am not sure there are words to describe the terror I felt at being alone, in addition to the overwhelming sadness from losing Jim on top of that.

This was not the first relative I had lost. My grandmother had died in my arms when I was 16 after suffering a heart attack at her home. My beloved father had died in a similar manner as Jim from lung cancer as well. I felt like I was so broken, so utterly alone and torn apart, I could see no way I would ever emerge from this intact. As I sat there in the house I could never imagine how I could ever be happy again.

Chapter 2

Childhood

In contrast to my marriage, I had a perfect childhood, almost storybook. I grew up in a house that was always full of love and happiness. I am always perplexed by stories from my friends who complained about spending time with their families. I can think of nothing better than being with my family. My father had had one child from a previous marriage when he met my mother who had four children from her previous marriage. I resulted from that union about a year and a half later. I was spoiled and doted on by my older siblings and entire family. There were no "steps" or "halves" in my house. Once you were in our family, you were in. Blood meant nothing; it was the family and love that mattered. We were glued together into my perfect, quirky, unique family by love.

My childhood was filled with family vacations in a huge green passenger van that my father purchased so each child could have a window. We went to the Grand Canyon, Daytona Beach, West Virginia, and many places to visit friends and relatives. Dad and Mom figured if they left on vacations at 11 at night the kids would sleep for the first eight hours and they would have quiet. One of our famous family stories was when Mom was driving one night and Dad and all us kids were asleep. Apparently Mom missed an exit on the interstate and decided to back up to get to it. Five kids and Dad shot up to find out why mom was backing up. We always teased her about that. We went to Disney World often and had a huge collection of those A to E tickets you used to get on rides. We played board games together as a family and always ate dinner together. My house was always filled with laughter and kindness.

My father was a firefighter and that was ideal for a child growing up. He worked 24 hours on and 48 off. We spent the entire summer fishing in our boat together in the Gulf of Mexico. Once off Egmont Key, we spotted a hammerhead shark and we both jumped in with our snorkels to see it! I can remember no time in my life when I wasn't happy with my father. He never said an unkind word in his life to me or anyone else. He cried at sad movies, never raised his voice, and had the patience of a saint. I remember driving lessons in a 69 Volkswagen Bug. Learning to drive a stick was somewhat out of style then, but he insisted that all of his kids learn on a manual car. He sat in the passenger seat with a hand on the emergency brake getting jerked around while I learned to ease off the clutch. I am sure I panicked him more than once, but he never showed it. When I started dating, sometimes I couldn't get my boyfriend on the phone and I would find out he was out fishing with my dad. My friends always wanted to come play at my house where Dad would barbecue and make everyone feel at home. When someone thinks of a perfect dad, my father's picture should be next to the definition.

My mother was my father's soul mate. She had a great sense of humor, the most wonderful laugh, and the patience needed to raise six kids in a blended family and treat them all equally and with love. We spent many hours doing puzzles, talking, and reading. Although her fashion sense was somewhat of an embarrassment to me, we were always very close and enjoyed spending time together. My mother's major flaw was her intense fear of snakes, which is not a good phobia to have in snake-laden Florida. The look of horror on her face when she came home and saw me holding tiny ring neck snakes in our backyard was priceless. One poor black snake wandered past my mother's gaze one night and in her panic to hack it to death, she managed to cut our poor garden hose into quite a few pieces, while a very frightened black snake managed his escape. Many times during adolescence, mothers and daughters have conflicts and are not close. That never happened with my mom and me. I'm sure there were moments when we had the normal teen

29

daughter /mother angst, but it was minor. When someone tells me I'm like my mother, I just smile at that amazing compliment. She was the perfect mother, and I loved her.

And the siblings? Well, they were always there to take me to movies, build tent forts in the living room, watch scary movies on Saturdays, go to Disney World or the beach, so many fun times. As the youngest, I often did try to get one to "outbid" the other in who was going to take me where and who would play with me for the day or go to cool places. Siblings always have a special place in your heart. Dianne, the oldest, always took me to movies and we built the most incredible forts in the living room and watched scary movies in them all day Saturday. Next up was Karen. Karen and I loved to go to Disney World and other places. I can still see Karen's face lit up watching a parade down Main Street on one of our trips. John was my oldest brother. I have no memory of John living with us. My strongest memory is how protected I felt by my big brother who would have and still would do anything for me. Leslie was the closest in age to me, separated by ten years. She was married when I was young and I got to visit her all over the United States as she moved with her Navy husband.

My grandmothers had each lost their husbands less than a year before I was born. I was told by both of them, especially my Dad's mom, that I was born to make them happy and I experienced many days living with my Grandmother Leatherbury in her beach house being spoiled beyond all belief. I feel so sorry for children who don't grow up surrounded by love like I did.

Often times in the summer, I would go stay with my Grandmother Leatherbury in her house on St. Petersburg Beach. I think we might have giggled ourselves to death and we laughed over everything. We were doing word searches in the New Yorker and we would take turns finding silly words. To this day I can still hear us saying Alley OOOP, horseeee, HOG (in a deep voice here), and laughing ourselves sick. This made sense to no one but us and I'm sure it won't to you either, but every time I read this sentence I smile and can hear her voice clearly. We played Payday, the board game, and if I landed on Sunday, her rule was I would have to say "Sweet Sunday" and run around and give her a kiss. We had this love of food and one night after eating way too much, we started singing this song we made up about us eating Nutter Butters then laughing hysterically. I still smile every time I eat one of those cookies. I remember heading there for a weekend in the summer and we would devise plans to extend my stay. A weekend stay often blossomed into weeks as Grandma insisted to my parents that she just couldn't live without me helping her. Then we would giggle with glee when Mom and Dad decided to let me stay. Grandma let me go to a store alone for the first time. I remember pushing her cart up the coquina stone sidewalk, grocery list in hand. I felt so special and grown up. There were lunches at the Five and Dime, trips to Mass Brothers, and we got to ride the bus to downtown. I thought I had the coolest grandmother in the world. As she aged she could no longer live alone and moved in across the street from us. Now I could spend more time with her. One time when she was in the hospital, she and I would move the leads on her EKG just to have the nurses run in and be freaked out. Then we would laugh endlessly.

We hired an older lady to come and live with Grandma to help her out when she was past the point of living alone. She had emphysema and her health was quickly declining. On December 19th, 1984, I was 16. I was released from school early to go to work. I did not have to be there till 5:00 so had about four hours before I had to report. I decided to go see Grandmother. She looked especially happy to see me because she had Christmas presents for the family and wanted me to help her wrap them. Some things she had purchased, but many others were things of hers she wanted wrapped up. She then asked to go and visit the dog, Sage. I thought it was an odd request. She loved the dog, but was not big on petting her. I held onto her arm and we started the slow walk across the road. We had to stop frequently to let her catch her breath. We petted the dog, rested for a bit, and then headed back. Halfway across the road, she stopped, looked me in the eyes and said she was so sorry she wasn't going to make it to Christmas and didn't want to ruin it for me. I shrugged it off as just normal worry and I got her back home, kissed her and headed to work. I got off around nine and my parents were bowling. I noticed her helper was standing in the door so I rushed over and went in. Grandma was lying in her chair, eyes shut, slightly twitching. I moved to her side and kissed her on the cheek, holding her hand. I leaned over to her ear and whispered to her that I was there and loved her and held her. The second I said it; she stopped moving, got a peaceful look on her face and just slipped away. I felt her leave us and the pain lift. I'm sure some of these memories are fogged over by the intense emotions, but I am sure I felt her soul leave and give me a parting kiss on the cheek as she left. The paramedics got there and I was sitting outside leaning against a tree crying. Soon after when my parents got there. They took Grandma away, still trying to resuscitate her, but I knew she was gone. Death has its own look and that was the first time I had seen it and I knew it. Sadly I have seen death many times since then and the look is unmistakable. I know why death is personified in so many poems and stories. Death has a presence in the room that is inescapable. Despite the overwhelming grief I was feeling at my first loss of a loved one. I was comforted by the knowledge that I was with her and I knew she knew it. My family just enveloped me in love and support and I still think fondly of Grandma and smile whenever I think of her. I have her same quirky sense of humor and the ability to laugh at just about anything. What a great gift she left me.

My father took the loss of his mother especially hard. Dad cried at her funeral and my heart broke further seeing tears running down his face. I spent many hours with him fishing and just being there for him. We were both hurting, and sharing that grief brought us even closer. Although Christmas was tough that year, especially as we opened her presents, we remembered her with fondness and were comforted by the loving and positive memories that she left with us. We chose to remember her with happiness and cherish her memories. We made a choice to be happy and live our lives by remembering hers and all the wonderful experiences we shared with her. After all, we are who we are because of her.

My many cousins, aunts, uncles, and other supportive and loving family members enriched my childhood and made it one full of love and happiness. My mother was the eighth of fifteen children and I have approximately 65 first cousins. I think this love of family helped me endure the sadness of my grandmother's passing.

A counselor once asked me years later how my father dealt with anger, well he was rarely angry. I can never remember him raising his voice. I can still see her disbelieving expression when I said I rarely ever saw my father angry. He was the most even tempered, kind soul I have ever known. I had no clue how to respond to her questions asking how I got involved with someone so unlike my father and to this day I still don't. I suspect that counselors expect you to have some deep, dark family problems when you come to counseling, but honestly I couldn't think of a single thing.

The only blemish in my childhood was school, middle school in particular. I was a good student, tried hard and enjoyed learning, but I was overweight and had buckteeth up until ninth grade when I finally got braces. I was a target in the mixed-up, meanness known as middle school. What I remember most about middle school and the taunting and teasing that I endured there. One girl in particular, took great pleasure in calling me goofy and fat and availed herself of every possible opportunity to harass me. I also did not have the designer clothes and newest fashions popular in the 70's and didn't take care of my hair with curling, primping, and teasing. Hair and girl stuff weren't my priority and I took abuse on that from her as well. I remember coming home from school and just crying to my dog, wondering how I could endure middle school. One day years later while I was teaching 8th grade, I was talking with my students about hate when we were reading *To Kill a Mockingbird* and one of my students asked me if I hated anyone. I was surprised without even thinking I said the girl's name who had teased me. I have no idea what became of her and never saw her after middle school, but am still surprised by the hatred I still have for her. Bullying and teasing cause wounds that just never heal and are unforgivable. I still hate her.

The only joy of my middle school years that made it bearable and enjoyable were my friends. Donna, Dawn, and Paige, my closest amigas. I still am in contact with them. When someone asks me what was good about middle school, it was them. Crazy, fun, goofy, and growing up together and discovering who we were as we grew toward adult hood made a special bond. So even though I had to endure bullying and teasing, I made it through middle school because of my friends. I chose to focus on my friendships and not let the naysayers and negative influences in my life dominate me. Maybe someday I will be able to make the choice to forgive the "bully", and I do hope she had a good life, but I am not sure I could honestly forgive the pain she caused me. But bullies and name calling don't define who you are. Keep your positive influences close to you and surround yourself with people who support you and who are truly your friends.

Chapter 3

Now what?

As I sat alone in the house the day that Jim died my head was spinning. I was in denial, of course. Denial he was dead, denial that he had been controlling, denial he was angry, denial it was he and not I that caused the problem. I was waiting for him to tell me what to do, what to eat for dinner, what to watch on TV, what time to go to bed, what to do in general. I had this picture of him and our relationship in my head that we had a perfect marriage. It honestly took me six months to come to terms and realize things were not as rosy as I made them out to be and almost six years to admit to others and myself the full extent of the verbal abuse and control that he had over me. But as I sat there so soon after his death, I just felt lost and alone and scared. How could I live without him? I was even afraid to turn on the TV and watch a show I wanted to watch. I had not had the ability to do so in years.

My mother and siblings were on their way and would arrive tomorrow. Relief set in, finally someone to help me. I took two Tylenol PM and hoped to drift into a deep sleep, but that was not to be. Every time I nodded off, I would hear his breathing stop, him pulling the oxygen out, or alarms going off. I would literally leap from my bed before I was awake to try to fix the problem. Then when I realized where I was and that he was gone. I would be overwhelmed with sobs and sadness. This was to go on for months almost every night. As soon as my eyes closed I would hear his labored breathing and I would not be able to sleep.

So after my third day in a row with virtually no sleep, I opened the door and fell into my mother's arms. We were running late for the viewing and Sue Wilson, my friend from work was going to be there. True to her word, Sherry had found an Episcopal Priest. Jim did not want a funeral. He had requested just the two of us for a final goodbye, but my mother needed closure too. So I had asked Sherry to schedule a viewing. I headed off to the funeral home with my sister Leslie, brother Johnny, my friend Sue, and my Mom. We walked into the funeral parlor and the director said something to us and led us back to a room. I am eternally grateful to the funeral director who made Jim look like Jim again. He looked happy, peaceful, and like he was just sleeping. I had chosen his favorite clothes for him, nothing fancy, just what he usually wore. He looked good and I needed to see that.

I was not prepared for my mother's reaction. This hit too close to home for her after dealing with my father's death. She hurried to the couch clutching her chest in pain. My sister got her nitro pills into her. My brother and sister tended to her and Sue tended to me because at this point, I was having trouble standing up. The priest was a woman in flip flops and white robe. She read some things from the Bible I suppose although I don't remember. I stared at her red toenail polish and her flip flops and knew not a word of what she said. I read something I had written about Jim and our lives. Then just like that it was over. I said my final good bye and we went back to my house.

My mom was a cash kind of gal. She had wanted to pay for the funeral and cremation so had brought $1000 in small bills. She had placed this in her purse along with a $1000 or so for her, and about four packs of unopened cigarettes. She had placed this purse with a large shoulder strap on the floor while we talked. Well we have all heard the expression curiosity kills the cat. Well Flopsie, my 21 pound black and white cat, stuck his nose in there to investigate while we were talking. He lifted his head up, realized he was caught in the strap, and took off running with the purse swinging from his neck and $2000 in cash literally exploding out along with untold numbers of loose cigarettes. It took us five minutes to corral the cat. Much needed laughter ensued as we tried to pick up the money

(I found cash and cigarettes hidden around the house for a few weeks). My mother's purse was broken, which made my sister happy, she hated that purse. I would not have thought it was possible to ever laugh again. I realized then that you have to find your own happiness. You can't let sadness and grief dictate your life. I could mope around the house or enjoy laughter and try to figure out how to live my life alone. At this point it was a small sliver of happiness, but it would be the start of many. My happiness wasn't consistent progress, but full of ups and downs, good days and bad days, but always I came back to the cat with the money flying and realized that laughter and happiness felt good. It was the first spark of happiness I had felt in a long time.

Now my family is gone, my husband is gone, and here I sit. I took a week off work to settle insurance, paperwork, death certificates, canceling credit cards, and an unbelievable amount of paperwork that is hard to concentrate on and deal with when you are coping with grief and loss. Teaching middle school is crazy enough. I had to make sure I had my grief and anxiety under control before I had to teach again. Laws change from state to state, but in Georgia, debt is not assumed by the spouse if your name was not on the debt. Nor are things owned. So the Mazda I had driven was in my husband's name only and I had no right to it. The choices were to buy it back from Mazda, more than the car was worth, or just let them repossess it, which is what I did. We still had a 350Z that was Jim's, but my name was on it too, so I could drive it until I figured things out. I think it took the entire week just to get the ball rolling on things and many years later I still get debt letters, letters addressed to him, and birthday cards in his name from companies. The paperwork is unbelievable.

The guidance counselors from my school showed up to talk to me. I was just numb. In addition to losing my husband, whom I had been with since I was 19, I was now 38 and I hadn't made a single decision on my own in my adult life. To everyone else we had the perfect marriage and they didn't suspect the abuse and control I had endured. I turned on the TV to distract myself and was almost afraid to change it to a show I wanted to watch. He had always made all the TV decisions and usually we had to watch car or fix it shows. I tentatively turned the channel to something I wanted to watch. Jim hated listening to music so I had not even listened to music in years. So many things I had never thought of. I honestly can't remember every little detail of that week, only the emotions of fear, uncertainty, anxiety, lack of sleep, and just being lost.

Then after a week I realized that I didn't have to walk on eggshells all the time. I thought how nice it was to be able to watch TV that I wanted to and go to bed when I wanted. The pit of fear that I constantly felt in the pit of my stomach was ebbing away. Then I felt overwhelming guilt for feeling that way. My husband had just died and I was happy I could watch a TV show? Shouldn't I be grieving and sad? I had nightmares almost every night at this point. Jim was alive, the hospital made a mistake and we would go somewhere. Sometimes he would be angry, sometimes not. Then I would wake up and realize it was a dream and be devastated. I still have "Jim" dreams off and on and am amazed how real they seem. Often now they take the form of Jim being alive and telling me I can't do the things I am doing now that make me happy. You have to give yourself permission to be happy. Your loved one is gone and nothing you can do can change that. It would take me years to believe that it was okay to be happy and enjoy life when he was gone and not feel guilty about it.

School was rough the next few months. I was certainly not up to par and the kids just ate me alive. I found that maintaining order and discipline was very hard. I had students that were very sympathetic, however. I had never had my ears pierced because my husband didn't like pierced ears. One student suggested to me to go get them done, actually I think she dared me, so I did. One mother sent me food almost every Friday so I would have something to eat over the weekend .She also invited me to her house for dinner for a full traditional Filipino meal. I often continued the very bad habit at this time of eating fast food for dinner. I did not want to eat in a big house alone every night and Jim had so controlled my eating habits that it felt good to be able to eat whatever I wanted. I continued this habit for years.

Before I knew it, the school year had ended. This presented itself with another serious set of problems. I had no social life, no activities, no hobbies, and no friends. Jim and I had pretty much been homebodies, watching TV and playing video games. We had gone to festivals, Dolly Wood, and occasionally a walk in the park, but I wasn't comfortable going anywhere alone yet. I was still having trouble going to the grocery store alone and picking out foods. We had some insurance money so I bought paint and hired a 17 year old daughter of a teacher at school to help me paint the entire inside of my 3000sq foot tri level home. That kept me busy, along with having hard wood flooring installed.

By July, I knew I had to do something other than sit, so I joined the YMCA in Canton. That is the first major decision I had made in my adult life and a huge turning point that would lead my life in a new and exciting direction. In addition, I decided to pursue my doctorate in education, maybe to prove I wasn't as dumb and useless as Jim often told me I was. Things were starting to look up and I was getting some confidence being alone. I still slept with a light on, but not right in the room. Nightmares were still common, especially the ones where I could hear his raspy, labored breathing and I would awaken suddenly, trying to help him breath. But all and all I was smiling more often than not. I was seeing a counselor once a week to deal with things, but I was never honest with her about Jim. I still told everyone he was world's best husband. I was not yet even ready to admit to myself his flaws and this controlling nature. I was not around couples much so I really didn't have anything to compare it to. But I think I knew then how wrongly he treated me. I just wasn't ready to admit it. I was amazed when I saw married friends and the wives made choices sometimes and their husbands just smiled and were OK with that. And that was hard to take. How had I lived 15 years being totally controlled like that? Yet I still felt that he loved me and treated me well for the most part. I had not at this point admitted to myself how dysfunctional my life had been.

July 5th was our anniversary and on the 3rd, I was on the couch crying. I just couldn't imagine what I was going to do. I hadn't been out with friends in years, and still, with the exception of going to the Y, came home most days after work alone and just sat there with the cats watching TV. I heard a pitiful meowing and after checking all my cats and seeing they were okay, I opened the back door and in walked the most emaciated kitten on wobbly legs, all charcoal gray. He walked in sat down, looked at me as if to say, "Here I am." I scooped him up, took him to the vet, and called him Little Bit, for little bitty angel. He made me smile. At some point his legs had been broken and healed wrong and he still walks with a funny gate. He brought happiness and laughter to me as I watched him adjust to his new home. He couldn't have come at a better time.

Time marched on and I was moving through the stages of grief and learning to live alone. In the back of my mind I was starting to realize how abusive and under his control I was. One night a few months after he died I decided I had to get rid of his clothes. I often get something in my head and just have to do it; I can't wait on it or think about it. I just could not stand to see his clothes in the closet and drawers every day. So I packed everything in boxes and headed to the local charity thrift store. I carried them in, got a receipt and as I headed for the car. I broke down crying and was unable to stop. I was wracked with uncontrollable sobs as I realized I had just gotten rid of something as personal as his clothes. Some very nice lady saw me and sat with me on her tailgate for quite some time listening to me and reassuring me. We often hear about the bad in people, but there are way many more good people then bad. I have no idea who that woman was in Jasper, Georgia that day, but I hope she realizes how much of a difference her kindness made in my life. As I drove home I realized I had taken a huge step in moving on and making a life for myself. I had made another choice and taken a course of action to move on and be happy instead of wallowing in grief and staying stagnant in my life.

Chapter 4

Canyon Preparation and Planning

"A river seems a magic thing. A magic, moving, living part of the
very earth itself."
— Laura Gilpin

This book is a book of discovery, growth, healing, and finding my
place in a vastly changing world. Half of the book is my life story
and half is a journey I took as I wrote this book that so deeply
affected me and seemed to mirror my life journey. Some indulgence
is needed as we proceed through my life story and what I feel was a
second chance at life, found in the most unlikely of places and
circumstances, the Colorado River from Lee's Ferry to Pearce Ferry.

In 2014 I decided to do a bucket list trip and kayak the Grand
Canyon. Having fallen in love with kayaking as discussed later in
this book, I set about doing this with a group of friends and my
kayaking outfitter, Endless River Adventures. Seemed easy enough,
pack, get on a plane and go. But like so much in life things aren't as
simple as they appear and they don't always go like expected. The
trip was quite a sum of money and guiltily I put it on a credit card.
My friends were going on this trip and I wasn't going to miss out on
a chance of a lifetime. My life over the last eight years seemed a lot
like the mighty Colorado to me; muddy at times, turbulent,
unpredictable, daunting, and yet possessing a beauty and wildness
that made life worth living. It seemed like the perfect fit for me. I
was feeling like I needed a substantial change in my life. I was tired

of teaching and was feeling the urge to roam, more and more lately. Unsettled in my surroundings, kayaking 280 miles of the Grand Canyon seemed a perfect place to think, get away, and try to get some perspective on things.

I started researching all I could about this river and its rapids. I read the book *The Emerald Mile*, which tells about the fastest run through the Grand Canyon and a record that is still held by that mighty wooden dory. I fell in love with the river and its people through that book. I felt like I was with Powell making his voyage and couldn't wait to see Separation Canyon where three men disappeared forever and were never heard from again. Crystal Rapid was described with such intensity I was full of wonder and awe at the thought of seeing such a rapid that magically appeared overnight in a flood and was semi-tamed by one some twenty years later. I would soon be there in the legendary Crystal Rapid. I would hear the thunder of Lava Rapid, and see the beauty of the canyon and its mysteries. We were going with Hatch River Adventures and would have two motorized rafts with us catering the food and bringing the camping gear. I sought advice from friends who had been there, wanting to be as prepared as possible. When traveling, I am not a spur of the moment kind of gal. I like to plan, pack, repack, and be prepared for all contingencies.

The first advice I got was sand. It would be everywhere they said, in everything, on everyplace, inescapable. My reply was I'm from Florida, I grew up in sand. Sure they said. You wait. Grand Canyon sand is unique.

Next: diaper rash cream. Why? Apparently hiking around in wet board shorts leads to rashes in odd places. I was skeptical of this one, but packed a bottle, along with baby wipes to clean up a bit.

Salve and lotion. Being from Florida, when I think heat, I think humid. The concept of a hot, dry desert heat was so foreign to me. I couldn't even picture it in my head, but I bought the suggested products and some Lubriderm and extra lip balm.

Pack as few clothes as possible, you won't need them. Trust me they said. Three pairs of river clothes and a cotton shirt at night. So I packed light, at least clothes. My growing back of lotions, creams, and first aid stuff weighed far more than my clothes bag eventually did. This affectionately became known as my lotions and potions bag.

The most common piece of advice I got was that The Grand Canyon would change me in such a way that I would always miss it, always long to be back sleeping under the stars, and feel a longing to return. There is a kind of peace and tranquility that cannot be explained, but would have to be experienced. Having had nothing but the lack of tranquility in my life in recent years, that was something I was eager to experience. Twelve days living in the wild, no wifi, phones, electronics, deadlines, lesson plans, Facebook, just good old nature at her best and in the company of good friends. I am one of those people always checking her phone, but I was uncharacteristically excited by the prospect of not looking at my phone for almost two weeks. I selected a few books and was looking forward to the solitude of the canyon.

Flying with a kayak and paddle is no small undertaking and to be honest virtually impossible. Airlines that will take skis, surfboard, golf clubs, and all kinds of heavy and breakable gear, will not take a 45 pound piece of durable plastic designed to drop off huge waterfalls, hit rocks, and not break. I have not and will never see the logic behind this. So I arranged for my friends Keith and Andrea to transport it for me since they were driving out and booked a flight to Las Vegas, starting point for most Grand Canyon trips. I would arrive at 10:00 am on Tuesday, July 15th, meet up with friends and the whole lot of us (18 strong) would be in a charter van following a truck full of kayaks for a five hour journey to Cliff Dweller's Lodge.

I had been planning this trip for almost a year by reading books, looking at videos, studying maps. Yep. I was super prepared. There would be no surprises on this trip. I took multiple kayak lessons so my skills would be sharp and my confidence high and took my favorite kayak, my trusty Wavesport Diesel. I double and triple checked my packing, made sure everything was organized and would be easy to pack in the dry bags. The best laid plans of mice and men is some part of a famous quote that might apply to this part of my story. No matter how well you plan, nature has a way of getting the last laugh and unfortunately for me (or fortunately as it would turn out in the end) the Grand Canyon and Colorado River had their own way of doing things that cannot be learned about in a book or planned for.

Just as in life, mine especially lately, you make these plans, set your goals, and are so sure that life will cooperate and you will get what you expected. However, sometimes life, nature, and vacations have their own plans that don't fit in your perfect plans. The trick is to accept these changes, embrace them, and look at these unexpected turns of events as a positive, not a negative. Some of the best things in life come about in the most unexpected of ways.

Chapter 5

Mountain Biking

My first summer alone I got this bright idea after taking spin classes that riding a bike would be fun. Now I'm from Florida and any biking I had done had been on flat land. So I read about the two kinds, mountain or road biking, and decided I would try the mountain biking. I am not sure why I thought "mountain biking" would be flat, but somehow in my Florida brain this is what I thought it would be like. Now a note on my physical characteristics, I am not small to put it politely, I have exercise induced asthma, and as a child had mitral valve prolapse and atrial septic defect in my heart. I was under no more heart restrictions, but still, these three characteristics do not lend oneself to heavy physical activity, but I was undaunted. I was determined I would no longer be this timid, shy, quiet woman. I marched into a bike shop to inquire about purchasing a mountain bike. The first shop I went to was not encouraging and they weren't helpful in anyway. I could tell by the looks they gave me they thought someone of my size and physical skill level wound never be able to mountain bike. So I gave up on that crazy idea.

A few weeks later, a sick cat led me back to my vet, Dr. Mike McGhee, an avid outdoorsman. I told him about the bike incident and he suggested I go see Mike Palmeri, who owns Cartecay Bike Shop in Ellijay, GA. He was a great guy and would hook me up with people to bike with. The next weekend, I got up the guts to walk in the shop after feeling so humiliated in the first one. I knew the second I met Mike that I would like him. He was a firefighter like my dad and had this wonderful, fun, outgoing, welcoming personality. Mike was the first person I credit with starting me on the road to recovery and turning me into the confident, happy person I would become. I am so thankful for meeting Mike, because in a way, everything that happened in my life after that was positive resulted from our meeting. You know the book *The Five People you Meet in Heaven?* I think both Mikes would be in my five people. They were put in my path to lead me down the right direction and both have been there many times for me in my life journey. Mike P. told me about bikes, helped me pick one out, outfitted it for me and told me about clothes I would need. Best of all he told me there were some women who road and that they are going out next Saturday on a beginner trail! I didn't know it then, but the women Mike would introduce me to would be the first really good tried and true friends I had had since middle school.

After the bike purchase I met an instructor at the Y who wanted to take me out for my first ride! We were going to a trail in Woodstock called Blanket's Creek. Now there are things in life that you look back on and think, "Well that wasn't very bright." That day was one of them. Being a Florida girl, my bikes had come from K Mart and we didn't have gears. Why would you need them? My idea of a hill as a kid was the teller lane at the bank that had an incline on it. I don't know what I was thinking as I headed out on that trail or what I expected, but it wasn't what I got. What I got was a single track with roots, trees, rocks, sand, mud, and HILLS. Yes hills real ones, with climbing. I almost passed out. And then came the bleeding. I kept smacking into trees and falling over roots. I fell three times and had nice crimson blood streaking down both legs when we finally made it to the parking lot. I wasn't sure if I liked it or not, but I felt alive! Invigorated. I had done something brand new that my husband never would have allowed. It would have been too dangerous. My husband was so cautious and worried about me getting hurt that he had never allowed us to do anything. Even though we met while Scuba Diving, he wouldn't let me do that again to protect me from getting injured. I have never been so wrong about an activity before I tried mountain biking. It wasn't what I expected, but I loved the adrenalin and feeling alive! Except for fishing and going to the beach, I had been an inside gal for most of my life. Now I was a mountain biker, riding through the woods, feeling the wind on my face, the dirt under the wheels, the blood on my legs, and the fear I was going to break every bone in my body. I was hooked.

Saturday came and I could barely contain myself. I was going to go mountain biking with a club. I still faced the self-doubt that I was going to screw everything up and someone would be mad at me. I also was worried about being out of shape that the ladies would not want to bike with me. It took a lot for me to drive there to meet them. I met Collin and Gail and they were to become my first really great friends since high school. They all eagerly greeted me and assured me that they would help me and would love to bike with me. We loaded up the bikes and headed to Woodring Branch trail in Ellijay. This is a round loop that can be ridden each way so we could all go at our own pace. When we arrived all I noticed were the trees. I was still kind of roughed up from my last encounter and was not wild about so many new scars. I asked them if there were trees on this trail. I was not encouraged by their laughter and smirks. I still could not control the bike well and although I was told this was a round trail and I could not get lost, I quickly found myself alone in the woods on a bike. I hadn't been alone anywhere much and certainly not in the woods. Every horror story imaginable crept into my mind and I was sure I was lost, four miles couldn't possibly be that long. Then from out of the woods some of my new friends, Kevin and Mary, appeared and assured me I was on the right track and almost to the end. Yep, I had to walk some from lack of muscle and excess fear, but I did it! Some of them did two laps and we didn't stay together, but I had fun and felt part of a group. We hung out at the parking lot for a while and for the first time in a long time I could see the life I could have, one with friends, the outdoors, new challenges, and most importantly happiness.

Collin, Gail, and I became good friends. We biked together frequently and many weekends I did group rides with them and groups out of the Cartecay Bike Shop. Eventually Kit joined our group. The four of us rode together almost every weekend and I was so pleased to have friends again. Soon I decided I was ready for clipless pedals, which is really a misnomer because you are clipped in to the pedals with them. I was going to be a better cyclist and I need the extra lift on the hills they would provide. I put my bike on a trainer and tried out the pedals making sure I could release them if needed. Gail's 14 year old son, Jeremy, agreed to take me out to Bear Creek Trail for my maiden ride. This trail starts with a climb on gravel roads. Up we went, I was surprised at how good I felt, the extra lift. I was feeling quite cocky. This wasn't hard at all. Then I got a bit tired and tried to stop, but I could not get my feet out and I slammed hard into the gravel. After four more falls, I decided to reevaluate my position on clipless pedals. Jeremy was being very supportive, but I just could not stop falling and had lost the skin on my shins, blood seeping down. I limped back to the bike shop, where Mike suggested a pedal a bit easier to get out of than shimanos, and I still ride with the new pedals. I learned a lesson then. Just because you try something and miserably fail, you just don't give up. Find an alternative that will help you succeed.

So less than a year from the death of my husband, I have now bought a mountain bike, met some great friends, and am outdoors for the first time in a long time. I am still having trouble making some decisions, but I don't beat myself up when I have troubles or am afraid to try new things. The outdoors has a way of healing you and the fresh air is just good for your soul. The exhilaration and adrenalin you get from riding the bike is complemented by the birds singing, clear blue skies, mud on your face, fresh air in your lungs. I remember times I would trail behind the group, stop the bike to rest, and just be utterly amazed at how wonderfully beautiful the woods are. I had never seen them like this or been in them. Every sound, smell and sight just is almost indescribable. It just makes you feel glad to be alive.

Chapter 6

Grand Canyon, The Journey: Flight from Atlanta Airport to Cliff Dwellers Lodge in Marble, AZ

"All journeys have secret destinations of which the traveler is
unaware."
— Martin Buber

July 15, 2014: The day was finally here after so many months of planning and dreaming. I got a ride to Marta with my friend Lisa and headed off to Atlanta Airport, duffel bags in tow. I am known as a sky miles schemer. I am always looking for new deals to earn free trips and I had scored a first class free flight on AirTran to Las Vegas, Nevada, starting point for most Grand Canyon Adventures. I settled on the plane and before I knew it I was in Vegas. As we were coming in for a landing I looked out the window and could see the Grand Canyon. I knew that I would be seeing it close from the inside, but seeing it from the top filled me with so much happiness and excitement. I was not a normal tourist glimpsing it from afar, but would be part of it for twelve days.

Now from what I could gather, Las Vegas was as far away from my vacation dreams of the Grand Canyon as possible. Lights, noise, gambling, tons of people are just not my ideal vacation. We had a three-hour wait for the shuttle, and I located my friends who had come in on a different airline. Securing a table in a restaurant, we started sharing our excitement for the upcoming trip. Tom, however, could not get out of Vegas quick enough. "I hate Vegas," was heard frequently. To be honest, we were all eager to get out, except Carli. All of 18, Carli wanted to gamble, which is a problem because you have to be 21 to gamble. But we were undaunted. Finding a slot machine kind of isolated I stuck $20 in so she could see the fallacy of gambling, how quickly that money would be gone. I thought that $20 was well worth the sacrifice to impart such knowledge to Carli. We played a bit and were down to $15 when she saw a slot machine with a horse on it and suggested we play that. So I cashed out and we moved there. I explained that you could pay more lines and a higher bet at greater risk but also greater profit so she selected a high bet. "This won't take long," I thought, as I hit the button. Sure enough lights, buzzers, and we were now $50 richer. Since my first lesson on the ills of gambling clearly didn't work, I was determined to show her the other lesson of "cash out when ahead." I offered to split the profit with her but she declined. So much for that lesson.

Our friends who had driven were staying at a nearby casino because they got free parking. Soon Tom, Carli, Lola, and I had met up with Matt, Jen, and Meghan, all of whom I knew. When I saw a new person, I said, "Oh, you must be Meghan's Mom!" to which she replied, "My name is Nancy, but I'm always known as Meghan's mom" in an exasperated voice. For the rest of the trip, Tom insisted on calling Nancy "Meghan's Mom". We were that kind of group. After being joined by our other friends, we boarded a charter bus following a truck pulling a trailer bulging with kayaks. In total we were 3 non kayakers who would raft and 15 kayakers. Quite the group.

I was almost bursting out of my seat with excitement. My very good friends Andrea and Keith, were on the bus, along with my almost daughter, Zoe, as well as Craig, Danny and his dad and a few other friends. I had known just about everyone on the trip but the legendary Art and Kari. Endless River Adventures is a smaller outfitter so the regular customers know each other and stories of Art and Kari had been told on Ecuador and Costa Rica trips for years. Art is Kari's father and I knew I would love the two of them

50

from the moment I met them. Both greeted me with a hug and hello like we had been friends for years. Their smiles and enthusiasm for the trip and being in our group were contagious. We had a long five hour ride ahead of us and we were super excited to get on the way to Cliff Dwellers Lodge in Marble, AZ.

The normal foolishness and conversations that occur on a bus of excited like-minded travelers ensued on this trip. I had never been out west and was amazed at the scenery. My eyes were accustomed to lush green forests, mountains, or beaches, not this landscape. Although desolate might be a good description I found beauty everywhere in that landscape and was amazed I would soon be living in it away from civilization for twelve whole days.

We passed through Needles, AZ, and I couldn't help but look for Spike, Snoopy's brother, out among the tumbleweeds and cacti. No one knew what I was talking about when I said, "Hey, look out for Spike!" After what seemed a much shorter trip than I thought, we pulled into Cliff Dwellers Lodge. After exiting the bus we were given hotel keys and told to enjoy dinner when we could. We would meet at 8:00 am the next morning, be given our dry bags, check our alcohol and beer purchases for the trip, and get orientation. I headed to the room I'd share with Carli and unloaded. Carli, Zoe, and Kari decided that scaling the mountain behind the hotel was a great idea. I headed to the restaurant for a beer. I had a feeling that twenty people ordering food in this small diner might be a bit of a problem. The waitress was on her second day working and was very polite getting first our drink orders then the food. Funny how when you are on vacation, relaxing with a beer, the service isn't slow, it's just right, allowing for chatting, wandering, and getting to know each other. Word was spread that one of our rafts was out over by the Hatch Warehouse so I headed over with friends to check it out. I had never imagined a 36 foot motorized raft and wow, it was big. We facebooked a picture of all of us on it.

After having dinner watching the sunset, we set off to bed. It had been a long day and tomorrow we would be paddling the Colorado River starting at Lee's Ferry. There are things you dream about and hope for and kayaking the Grand Canyon is certainly something that most kayakers dream of. To be here so close to Lee's

Ferry surrounded by friends, about to embark on a journey of a lifetime was hard for me to fathom. Was I the same person that just eight short years ago had never camped, kayaked, done anything adventurous, traveled, or gone anywhere alone? I fell asleep with a smile thinking that if you want something bad enough, work hard enough, and surround yourself with people who build you up and support you there is literally nothing in this world you can't do. I felt surrounded by people who I knew would be there for me and make this journey one that would always be remembered. This wasn't a simple vacation for me. It almost felt like the culmination of everything I had become over the last eight years, the kind of person I wanted to be, confident and an adventurer. Life has a way of taking you on unexpected journeys and I was about to start just such a journey. Nothing I could have done could have totally prepared me for the majestic, wild nature of the Colorado River and the Grand Canyon.

Chapter 7

Backpacking, Camping, Hiking

Collin owned a backpacking shop. I decided I had to make up for lost time and backpacking and hiking sounded like a good idea. So I signed up for a day hike to Jack's River Trail. Off I went on a six mile round trip daypack in my new hiking boots and daypack. Once again my Florida upbringing led to a surprise. Trails in North Georgia were not flat. They went up and down. A lot. They were also not paved or gravel, there were sticks, roots, rocks! I was much winded when we finally reached Jack's River, which presented me with a unique problem I had not thought of. I had to pee. Now this doesn't seem like a problem to most of you, I am sure, but somehow in my 38 years of living I had never had to pee in the woods and not in a toilet. I wasn't entirely sure how or where to go. I was having a bit of a panic attack at this point. How do you ask someone "Excuse me? How do you pee in the woods?" I finally was so desperate I wandered off behind a tree and set to the difficult task of peeing behind a bush for the first time. That memory kind of seared itself into my psyche. I thought I would never get over the trauma which is really funny. I think I pee outside more than inside in the summers now.

On my way back to the group, I looked around. There were no signs of civilization, just the people in my group, blue sky, water trickling, birds chirping. I just sat down and could not believe I had not spent more time in the woods. How much I had missed. I decided then that the outdoors was for me. No more TV, video games, and sitting around. I was happy and at peace. I was going to get out there and enjoy this great outdoors, which led me to my first backpacking trip.

Now in the movies when people backpack they are smiling in matching clothes, unless it is a horror flick, and then they are running for their lives. I was to find out that was not how backpacking was in the real world at all. I went to Collin's store, bought a backpack, sleeping bag and pad, the works. I was ready. Collin had a water purifier and stove and I picked out my freeze dried dinner. It was decided to do Panther Creek Falls since it is only about four miles in. Four miles, easy. I had already learned that nothing in North Georgia was flat, so I had bought trekking poles, which would make it easier. My pack weighed in at 25 pounds. We set off and after five minutes it was apparent to me that I was not in good enough shape to hike four miles downhill and uphill with a pack on my back. Being overweight, asthmatic, and a couch potato for most of your life does not exactly prepare you for backpacking, but I kept on going, slow and steady. At one point the trail was so steep I thought I would have to take off my pack to get down it but down I went, legs shaking, and I was sure blisters were forming on my feet. We walked for about four hours and came to one of the prettiest places I had ever seen. We were at the top of Panther Creek Falls, a short walk from the campsite we had an unbelievable summer view of the Cohutta Wilderness Area. The water went by us through a meandering river under the rocks we were sitting on and over the falls and disappeared into the woods below us.

Now if you backpack you need a tent, which I had purchased, but never set up or slept in. In fact it occurred to me I had never slept anywhere, but in a bed. Even in girl scout camping we had slept in cabins with electricity and bathrooms. I picked a spot underneath a huge tree, flat, no rocks, perfect and pitched my first tent. I crawled in with a sense of pride and wonderment. My home. I had carried it, erected it, and now was going to sleep in it, in the woods. It was a bit chilly that night so we built a camp fire and then I learned how to use a propane backpacking stove! I am still amazed at how good freeze dried backpacking food tastes in the woods, the only place it does taste good actually. After our meal and some hot chocolate we walked to the top of the falls sat on a rock and watched the sun set over the mountains.

Walking back with my newly purchased headlamp, it occurred to me. It was dark, very dark, incredibly dark. And there were noises in the woods, lots of them. A new thought occurred to me. It was going to be dark and I was in a tent in the woods. I was not the adventurous sort of person at the time and I was starting to get a bit apprehensive. This was followed by Collin explaining that we needed to hang food from a tree away from us, so the bears wouldn't come and get it. Bears? Really? I was feeling very nervous. We sat around the campfire and it started to rain, so we all climbed into our tents. I can almost hear the outdoors people saying things like "rain on a tent sounds so pretty" or "love that rain smell."

Me? I was not thinking that at all. I was thinking I am in a tiny two person tent made of nylon under a big tree alone in the woods with bears. And just about the time I slunk into my sleeping bag it started to lightning and thunder like crazy. I'm from Florida, so I know lightning. Now pitching my tent by a great big old tree did not appear to be overly wise. I popped some Tylenol PM for sleep and very achy muscles and finally started to drift to sleep. Amazingly, I slept better than I had since my husband died.

So now after many backpacking, hiking, and camping trips under my belt, I have come to the conclusion that there is nothing better in this world than being in the woods, especially alone. Yes, I hike alone. I always leave my itinerary with someone, but there is just something magical about exploring things on your own, no one to talk to, looking around, finding peace. Love it.

Now a further note on bears, I appear to be a bear magnet. I have seen them camping, mountain biking, kayaking, so many of them I almost am surprised when I don't see them. Coming up on a black bear is such a special, unique thing. I feel so blessed I have seen them. Most of the time I see their back end as they take off, but twice I've almost nailed one on a mountain bike. I shudder at that thought, and once I came upon one on my bike, stopped, and he was sitting maybe 100 feet in front of me eating berries, his butt in the trail. "Shoo bear," I yelled. He looked at me as if to say "Yeah, right." Well I knew what to do then. I turned around and headed back down the trail. "Happy berry eating, bear."

My city dwelling friends are amazed when I tell them this. I think they are convinced every critter in the wild is out to get you. Mind you, these people live in Atlanta and other big cities, nothing at all dangerous there, totally safe. I will take the bear. Although running over a snake while mountain biking and having it fly up at you snapping while your feet are clipped in is an experience I can live without. If more people would get out doors I am convinced they would be happier people.

Chapter 8

Grand Canyon Day 1:
Lee's Ferry to mile 19

*Sometimes luck is with you, and sometimes not,
but the important thing is to take the dare.
Those who climb mountains or raft rivers understand this.*
— David Brower

It is hard to explain the excitement of finally seeing Lee's Ferry, the Holy Grail of kayaking places. One hears whispers of this place, sees pictures of friends in their kayaks there on Facebook, and dare to dream that one day we will be there in our kayaks setting off into the chilly waters of the Colorado. I exited the van and felt such a surge of excitement that I could hardly believe I was here. I was as giddy as a small child at Christmas. I could see our rafts and would soon be meeting the boatmen, swampers, and kayak guide who would escort us on this journey.

I now had experienced dry heat, quite different from Florida humid heat. I felt as if my skin was cracking under the intense sun as I started unloading and reloading on the raft. We all milled around in a sea of kayaks, dry bags, our two enormous rafts and rafts from other companies. Then I met Dave, our trip leader and kayak guide. One look at him and I could tell he had many Grand Canyon trips under his belt. His kayak hadn't been in production for years, a Wavesport Z, slicey and small. It was not the kind of boat you would think would make for good rescuing. I wasn't sure this guy could get to me in huge waves in that boat. That thought in my head was probably the most blatant reason why you should never ever prejudge people. As I was to find out all too quickly, Dave's rescuing abilities were unsurpassed by anyone I had ever met. More stories on that later.

I wish I had recorded Dave's description of the rapids and what we were heading into. I was accustomed to ERA's logic and ordered trips. Dave told it like it was. Rapids were huge and fun. Some of us would probably get a whipping and epic beat down in waves like we have never seen, but that's what we had come for right?

Now I am not known for my confidence, the opposite in fact. But I was so dang sure I was ready for anything this river could dish out. I was master of the Ocoee, I had been rolling and prepping all summer. How hard could a river be with only big waves and no rocks or technical moves? Seriously? Mother Nature as always has the last laugh there. Rivers have a mind of their own and don't care that I had worked hard and mastered skills. It was a wild and free entity and had its own plans for me.

Shortly after departure we passed under the Navajo Bridge. I couldn't believe I was here. The normal famed muddy waters were a crystal blue/green and icy cold, a sharp refreshing contrast to the 100 and up heat of the air.

Then I heard the telltale sound of a rapid coming up and my heart raced. "Just a riffle," said Dave. I, having never heard that term, asked what a riffle was. Just a small set of waves, not big enough to be a rapid no problem. Oh, no problem. Yep. So around the bend we go and here are these huge waves, some of the biggest I've ever seen. I started climbing up the waves and felt that roller coaster stomach lurch you get from dropping fast. I couldn't believe it, this thing would fit right in in the middle of the Olympic Section of the Ocoee. Not a rapid? What did the rapids look like? But it sure was fun. Then I got introduced to the next phenomenon of the Grand Canyon, eddies, boils, and eddy fences. In most rivers an eddy is a place of calm water, a safe spot. Not so much here. You had to plow your way through massive boils, squirrely water, and unstable whirlpools just to get in an eddy where you then became trapped unless you got back across the eddy fences. I soon learned to stay in the current. Lesson learned: Doesn't matter how well you think you are prepared, rivers and nature do their own thing in their own way and to go with the flow, pun intended.

I was getting in the groove of paddling. A long day for us is normally eight miles, here we would be pushing 20 and more. I had my first combat roll in a rapid called Soap Creek. Now I was on cloud nine, I was a great kayaker and had this river down! No swims or problems for me. I could roll in a huge wave train and have fun. And once again, the river won in a rapid called House Rapid. We scouted this one. I thought it looked easy, huge tongue and you just moved to the right side of the channel to avoid the huge pillow of water and hole. How hard could that be? There was plenty of time. So off I went and started to work right. Now this is easier said than done, I had no clue how fast that current was moving and how hard it was to move to the right. I never made it, I smashed into the pillow of water knowing I should be leaning into it, but just couldn't get myself to lean into that huge mass of water, so over I went. I tried to roll, but was unsuccessful and has my first swim on the Colorado. So when I surfaced, Dave was there immediately. The purpose of all those ropes I saw hanging of his boat became evident as I was clinging to one of them being dragged to shore. I could almost hear the river snickering as I swam to shore holding on to Dave's boat.

My confidence was slightly shaken, but one roll, one swim, not bad really for a river I have never been on before. We headed to mile 19 to camp for the night. My experiences in life have made me unsure of myself especially in unfamiliar situations. I often have anxiety to the point of not being able to function. But I always work through my fears, no matter how insurmountable they may appear to be. I have found with persistence, there are very few mental hiccups that you can't work through. I wasn't prepared for the fear and anxiety I felt at that first campsite. Where the heck did we camp and that was a loosely defined term. Camp was a cot that we had to set up on sand somewhere. I unwisely thought I should get away from the water. So I found this sandy spot by a tree (well kind of a tree), and attempted to set up this cot. Not happening. I tried and tried to set up that thing and finally Keith came to the rescue and up went the cot. I now discovered I was by red ants, lots of them. I grew up with fire ants, but these things looked like something out of Africa. Huge. Dave warned us anyone bit by one would be in excruciating pain for 12 hours. Nothing you can do, but soak in the cold water and wait it out. Luckily they weren't aggressive and would only bite if pinched or smashed. They also went to bed at dark. I sat on the cot trying to organize things. I will always be able to see that campsite in my head so clearly. It is seared into my memory as a panic washed over me. How in the heck could I sleep outside? What if something crawled on me? Snake? Lizard? Scorpion? I was imagining how I could live twelve days without any sleep. I felt like an idiot surrounded by people who were obviously in Heaven, and here I was sitting on the cot in the midst of an anxiety attack.

And just when I thought I couldn't get any more anxious, I met the groover. A groover is a toilet of sorts, a stainless steel bucket with a toilet seat. The park service prohibits poop from being left in the canyon so we all got to use the groover. I couldn't imagine sitting on that thing in the open trying to go. And where did the groover go? Well, it went right in the most scenic view possible, on the top of the bluff overlooking the river and canyon. The oddness of that still gets me. So when you had to use the groover to go number two, first you had to go to the river and go number one. Pee was in the river only, not the groover. Then you went to the hand washing station and picked up the "door". The door was a cushion you took with you to signal you were using the toilet and for everyone to not approach. I looked at that set up with trepidation. Wonder if I could hold it for twelve days? Would that be bad? Luckily I did not have to use the groover that night.

Dinner exceeded my expectations. We had appetizers of smoked oysters, okra, cheese, Brie, crackers of all sorts, and humus. We dug in like a pack of hungry wolves. We had put beer and soda in bags in the water so sat down to enjoy a cold beer with the feast. Dinner was salmon, green beans, potatoes, and a salad. This was not what I was expecting. Dessert was a cake baked in a Dutch oven. As we were finishing up our dinner, we got our first camp talk by Dave.

These talks were the highlight of the evening. Here comes Dave, with a piece of cereal box in his hand reading notes off the back. He told us day two were the roaring 20's, non-stop big rapids for 10-15 miles, super fun surf waves. We would love it. He told us about the history of the canyon, geology, and we couldn't wait.

By 8:00 the sun was setting and the stars came out along with the bats. I have never seen so many bats. They flew everywhere in intricate dances directly over our heads in a beautiful display. By 8:30 most of us were tired so we wandered down to the river to clean up a bit, brush our teeth, and hit the cot. It was still very warm as I lay down on that cot trying to wipe sand off me unsuccessfully with baby wipes. I knew that I must face my anxiety about camping like this, not like I had a choice. I was going to be doing this for 11 nights. I felt my heart racing as I put my head down on the pillow and looked up at the sky. There are not adequate words to describe what I saw. Blanket of stars is not enough to tell about the night sky in the canyon and I'm not convinced anyone, no matter how gifted a writer they are could adequately describe the night sky in the Grand Canyon. The sky literally pulses with lights, like it is alive and its only goal is to show off and try to better itself each night with its starry display. Bats continued to swoop around and at that point I thought I don't care what crawls on me. The scene I was witnessing was so breathtakingly spectacular. I felt pity and sorrow for all the poor souls in buildings who will never experience nature like this, at her best. In such an awe inspiring show, nothing man made could ever even come close to topping it. I have to admit I was still a bit nervous about sleeping out there, but before I knew it I was sound asleep. Often at home I worry about things and can't sleep, work, bills, money, teaching, whatever but not in the canyon. I have never in my adult life slept so well and soundly. I woke up with the sun the next morning more refreshed and peaceful than I have felt in a long time. Humans are meant to be a part of nature, not excluded from it. In nature we truly find peace and tranquility that we lose in the concrete jungles of our daily lives. If we spent more time outside away from wifi, phones, TV, and in the company of friends and nature, we would all be much happier people.

Chapter 9

First trip May 2007

Growing up I had always thought I would like to travel, but Jim didn't. In all the years we were married, we never stayed away from the house overnight. There again, I think he liked the control he had in our house. But for all his faults, he was an animal lover and couldn't stand to leave the cats alone all night. Alaska was on my bucket list, a place I had always wanted to go and explore. A little more than a year after Jim's death, I asked Collin to go with me for a week. She suggested Seward and camping. I was amazed how quickly things can get put together when you are planning on "roughing it." So we got a plane ticket, found a Bed and Breakfast in Anchorage for night one, and rented a car. We landed in Anchorage close to midnight and the sun was still up, kind of like dusk. I was so excited. I can still see so clearly my first view of Alaska. I felt like I had taken some huge leap into an unknown adventure. I was a traveler, not just any traveler, an adventure traveler, a label that would unknowingly apply to me later more than I could ever imagine. I had the travel bug and I was hopelessly hooked. I hadn't been on a plane or anywhere since I was a kid and I felt like a part of my life that had been missing was suddenly put back in place. My father and I had traveled to Europe when I was a teen, just the two of us. He had never been out of the country either. What fun we had. I felt like I was on an adventure like that, just going to unknown places and exploring. My father and I had always been two peas in a pod and I felt that side of me awakening from the second I stepped off the plane. It is hard to pinpoint life-changing moments when you realize you have crossed a line for the better and healing has occurred. As I stepped off the plane at Anchorage, this was one of those moments. I had been so confined by Jim for so many years, my freedom stifled. I took a deep breath of that crisp Alaska air and felt it course through me. I was freed.

We drove to an incredible B and B nestled in a small, suburban neighborhood. Our room was wonderful and although sleeping when it was light out was a challenge, we woke up the next morning refreshed and ready for our adventure. I can thank Collin for my love of fairly spontaneous, unplanned trips, which I personally feel make for the best vacations. There would be many more trips like this in my life, but it all started with this one and I am eternally grateful to Collin for awakening the travel bug in me. We set off from Anchorage with a map, hiking book, tent, sleeping bag, and knew we were heading towards Seward, but planning on impromptu stops along the way. We had no set plans or reservations. When we spotted a trail we got out and hiked it, saw a place to stay we stayed there, cool vistas or trails off the highway, we went exploring. We had brought our cook stove and picked up fuel and food to cook instead of eating out so much.

Our first big hike was to see Portage Glacier. This was the first time I had walked in snow too! I should point out this was the end of May/ early June. I was amazed at how cold it was in June and the rain made it feel colder. My Florida birth had not prepared me for places that could actually be cold outside of January and February. We bundled up in layers and rain gear and headed up the trail. The glacier has receded so much that a visitor center erected in 1986 to allow visitors to observe the glacier is now too far back to even see it from the center. You can take a boat ride in or hike. On a rainy, cold day we headed out across the snowy trail to see the Glacier. I am still utterly awed by seeing such a massive mound of ice that feels alive. We saw ice worms, tracks from many different animals, and snow. I still get excited by snow, for someone who never saw even a flurry till I was 16, snow is magical to me.

It is hard to describe glaciers to someone who has never seen one. Glaciers are not white. White sounds dull, which glaciers are assuredly not. They are sparkly, alive, blue, white, pearl, grey, brown, grey, and colors for which I have no name. They sparkle, breath, move, shift, and feel alive. I had no idea there could be so many shades of white and hues of colors. We hear about glaciers receding, but until you see it first hand, it is hard to imagine. Signs are placed along the trail where the glaciers were and where they presently are. I was amazed at how much it had receded and so quickly. An adventurous spirit was awakened that day and has continued to flourish and grow. I learned you don't need good weather to have an awesome, incredible vacation/adventure. You can choose to have fun anywhere, anytime, in any circumstances or weather. Sometimes you just have to dance in the rain.

Next stop was Moose Gap and we decided to stay in a cabin that night. I learned a new trick from Collin. If you show up at a motel late in the day, especially a small privately owned one, you can haggle for a room. I always thought motel room rates were fixed, but no. We got a great cabin with a deck overlooking the lake, for an insanely cheap price, half of what they had advertised. So we took out our camp stove and with the supplies bought in Anchorage we cooked spaghetti and had salad right there on the deck. I couldn't believe I was in Alaska enjoying such breathtaking scenery. Vacations can be inexpensive if you haggle a bit and don't eat out in restaurants so much. Plus I have to say, that might have been one of the best pasta dishes, I've ever eaten.

On the way to Seward, we had spotted a trail in the guidebook called the Ptarmigan Lake Trail. It was described as a moderate to strenuous 3.6 mile trail one way. We loaded our day packs and headed out on a brisk and sunny day. I had encountered black bears hiking, but I was concerned about grizzlies. So we made noise as we were hiking to make sure we didn't sneak up on one of them. Collin and I sang as we hiked. It doesn't matter if you have a good singing voice or not, just sing. The hike was incredible. There is something wonderful about walking in the woods, especially a place you have never been, wondering what's around the next bend, what you will see or experience. It's just amazing. The trail went mainly up along a creek. We were in a protected side of the mountain so the wind was minimal, but the air was still cool. I was glad I had layers on. After hiking for quite some time, we rounded a bend in the trail and the vista took my breath taken away. A turquoise lake sparkling in the midday sun was laid out in front of me. Many bald eagles circled overhead with their cries echoing throughout the valley and then the wind hit us fiercely. We were no longer protected from the wind by the mountain. We had descended into the valley, and it was freezing, but I didn't care, it was so indescribably beautiful. We found a spot right on the water with rocks on 2 sides to protect us from the wind and ate our lunch shivering. I don't remember eating much peanut butter before I started sports. Now I think I keep peanut butter companies in business and almost laugh with glee when they are "buy one get one free" in stores. It is the perfect backpacking and outdoor food. I don't think a PB&J sandwich ever tasted so good as it did that day sitting by the banks of Ptarmigan Lake with an unbelievable beauty.

Nighttime found us in Seward, a small coastal town. Since it was colder than we had anticipated, we found a hotel and once again scored a great deal on a room overlooking the bay in a great hotel. We had come here mainly for the hiking and Exit Glacier National Park. Once again we saw wooden signs marking the spot where the glacier had once been and I was amazed at how far it had receded in such a short time. Exit Glacier was different from Portage Glacier. It attached to the Harding Ice Field system and was huge. It had a totally different characteristic to it. We could walk right across the terrain reminiscent of the moon and just reach out and touch it. Glaciers feel alive somehow and you can't help but wonder what secrets it holds in its frozen river system. We spent a few days here hiking around and even walked up the Harding Ice Field Trail, which amazingly was covered in ice and snow in June. This presented a new problem; I'm not really experienced at walking on ice and snow. As we scrambled up rocks and slippery wooden planks, my newfound adventurous spirit was severely tested with this ice -coated plank that went over the top of a waterfall without any kind of handrails or protection from a long, hard fall. I inched my way across the precarious makeshift bridge with a pounding heart. Collin, naturally, took a picture of my fearful face as I crept across. Then we started going up and up a snow filled trail. The entire hike is only eight miles round trip, but this was made very difficult by the snow which quickly became waist deep. We had reached an overlook where we could see the glacier and once again I was overwhelmed with the majestic views. Then a man who looked like someone out of *The Call of the Wild* came running down the hill saying, "Grizzly bear, the largest tracks I have ever seen and they are fresh." We decided to turn around then. But before we headed down, it occurred to me that I had never made a snow angel and now seemed like as good of time as any. So I put down my hiking poles, got in position and leaped backwards onto the trail into a huge pile of snow. Then I learned that snow is slippery and where I chose to do my first angel was a sloped trail, not flat. I shot down the hill like an out- of -control rocket, sliding at a high rate of speed as Collin laughed. I came to a rest against a rock where I then proceeded to make my snow angel, despite the fact that Collin's giggling could still be heard. But I had made my first snow angel. Laughing at yourself is a very important skill and sure makes life more enjoyable, especially for those that witness your silliness.

The only touristy thing I wanted to do was go on a whale watching bay trip. We found a boat and noticed everyone was bundled up. We bought extra rainproof hooded fleece lined jackets. To say it was cold on the boat is the understatement of the year. We were on the bow of the boat pelted by rain and sleet, but I hardly even noticed. There were whales everywhere. There were so many Orcas and Humpbacks that we had to stop the ship numerous times to avoid them because The Marine Mammal Protection Act prohibits people from chasing or getting in the way of whales. We had to stop so we didn't hit one and allow them to be unmolested in their travels through the bay. The humpbacks were tail slapping and surfacing out of the water, and there was a juvenile one tucked up tight against its mother. The orcas came by in pods and I took pictures of their dorsal fins, which I later sent in and got their history. They can tell you their age and life history from reading the dorsal fins. The Orcas interact with you. On more than one occasion as I leaned over the railing to look at them, I was greeted by one looking back at me. How amazing to stare into the eye of a wild orca and gaze at him as he gazes at you. What was he thinking? One cannot possibly realize how much good, beauty, and happiness is in our world until you stand in the presence of a pod of whales and have the fortune to exchange glances with one.

We were on our way to see a glacier that comes into the bay off the Harding Ice Field Trail. I really hoped to hear and see one calve. The captain parked the boat in a valley with sheer rock cliffs on the side full of black bears and a wall of ice in front of us. There was a constant crackling, settling, shifting noise permeating throughout the valley, but no calving. Other captains left, but our captain said to watch a certain spot. She had been doing this a while and was certain from the noises that a huge piece would calve soon. We all were quietly watching as the crackling got louder and louder. Then we saw it. A huge sheet of ice was shifting. A noise, which was a combination of cannon fire, gunshots, and explosions started to fill the canyon, increasing in volume as the ice shifted more and more. Then a huge sheet of this ancient glacier started to slip off the main glacier in slow motion. Finally it slid off and hit the water with a thunderous crash and a huge series of waves. The noise in that cavern cannot be explained to someone who has never heard it. I stood there unable to even speak. It was one of the most impressive displays nature can show you, and I felt honored to be in the presence of such a wondrous, powerful event.

We had not been camping due to the rain and cold, begging the night manager at the hotel for a discounted rate every night successfully. Finally on our last night in Seward, it was warm and clear, so we set up our camp in Exit Glacier Park. I had seen bears galore, but not a moose. There is almost 24 hours of daylight in Alaska in the summertime. A kind of hazy twilight comes around 2:00am, but it is quite light out the rest of the time. At 11:00 at night and wide-awake in the midnight sun, we headed off for a hike to find me a moose. While we did not see a moose, we did come across a very startled porcupine who scurried across the trail in front of us and ran up a tree shivering in fright. We saw lots and lots of bears, but still no moose. After returning to our tent, we finally put on some eye masks and slept peacefully in our tent. We woke up to copious amount of fresh moose pellets all around our tent. We must have had a night time visitor and I missed my moose. How can something so large move so quietly that we never heard it? Fun activities don't have to be relegated to any set schedule. When an opportunity for fun comes up, you have to seize it and jump on it even if it's the middle of the night.

We headed back to Anchorage and found a couple who were leaving for the night and owned a bed and breakfast. They graciously let us stay anyway and we had their entire house to ourselves! The next morning we fixed breakfast and set off to explore Anchorage and I finally got to see my wild moose right by the airport of all places.

Our flight back was so memorable it has to be included in this memoir. Collin and I had been going non-stop and the 24 hours of daylight had taken a toll on our sleep. Our plane was leaving around 11:00 pm and as we settled into our seats I took one Tylenol PM and she took two. This would have worked out fine except as the plane gunned it to take off down the runway, we came to an abrupt stop. I tried to wake up a groggy Collin. Something was wrong with the plane, and we would have to switch to a new one. We virtually supported each other through the airport in our stupor to the next plane. We were sound asleep until Houston. With only 30 minutes to connect flights, we were amazed when we made it. I expressed my fear to Collin that there was no way our luggage made it.

"Probably not," she responded. "Doesn't matter. What a great week we had right? Our luggage will catch up with us." Lesson learned. Don't sweat the small stuff when travelling. And actually our luggage was on the plane

So in only a year since the death of my husband, I had gone from someone with no friends, isolated, unable to go anywhere alone, with terrible self-confidence issues to mountain biking, hiking, backpacking, and travelling with a friend to Alaska with a fairly unplanned itinerary. Sometimes things happen in our lives that shape us in negative ways. The trick is to overcome those things and turn them into new beginnings. Many people had recommended anti-anxiety drugs or anti-depressant drugs for me after my husband died. I resisted and turned instead to the healing power of friendship and the great outdoors to deal with my overwhelming grief and sadness. I chose to make the right choice and to be happy and surrounded myself by people who would help me make that choice a reality. I was amazed at how the quality of my life changed when I started socializing and going outside. I still have some moments of anxiety, but they are becoming more infrequent. When I left Alaska, I knew I had fully caught the travelling bug. If someone had told me then how much solo traveling I would do in the upcoming years, I wouldn't have believed it. Travelling is just good for the soul and revitalizes you.

Chapter 10

Grand Canyon Day 2:
Mile 19 to Mile 50

There's nothing . . . absolutely nothing . . .
half so much worth doing as simply messing around in boats.
— Kenneth Grahame, *The Wind in the Willows* (River Rat to Mole)

I woke up from my first night in the Canyon invigorated with that feeling one only gets from a deep night sleep. I also felt relieved and proud of myself that I was getting more comfortable with the sleeping and living arrangements. I had persevered and worked through my anxiety and felt stronger and more confident because of it. I had never had anxiety as a child. Those feelings came from my marriage and adult issues. For me, time in the great outdoors, spending time with friends, and doing things I enjoy is the only drug I need. It might be the longer, more difficult path, but it is the right one for me.

However, now I was faced with the ever-pressing problem of using the groover. My initial plan of waiting for twelve days was obviously not going to work. I picked up the "door" and headed to find the groover, which was sometimes hard to locate in its secluded spot. This one was situated on the top of the rocks overlooking the canyon. The sun was just coming up and I could not believe this idealistic spot in which a toilet was placed. I hesitantly sat down and realized the stench was overwhelming for me and I couldn't stop gagging. There was a reason I had lived 46 years without changing a messy diaper. I have an insane gag reflex. What to do? I had a pair of nose plugs in my pocket, which did the trick. For the rest of the trip I went to the groover wearing my nose plugs. You do what you have to do. One more anxiety filled hurdle crossed. And I have to admit the first time I used a toilet back home, it was a bit boring staring at the wall instead of the sun coming up over the canyon and its sparkling rays hitting the river.

Hatch outdid themselves again with bacon, eggs (cooked the way you liked them), and a variety of fruit for breakfast. In my preparation chapter I mentioned I was warned about the sand. Once again words fail me to describe this phenomenon. Sand seems so simple to describe, but like everything else in the canyon, it is its own unique, spectacular, and grand thing. It is so fine and so deep that my calves hurt just to walk through it. It was the kind of sand that just felt good between your toes. This turned out to be a good thing since it was constantly there and just about everywhere else. After breakfast I was making final arrangements in my kayak, kneeling down beside it when Dave, our guide, asked me how I liked the camping. I looked up to answer and found him standing there totally naked, talking as nonchalantly as could be. "Great," I answered, "had a great spot, and slept like a log." Someday I hope to have the confidence to walk naked across the sand in view of the Colorado River. We packed up our cot and belongings stored into dry bags and formed the "chain gang" to load the boats. Everyone gets in a long line and passes the things down the line till the rafts are totally loaded and secure.

The water at this point was still a crystal blue. I was happy not to be experiencing the muddy brown Colorado I had heard so much about. My mood was as beautiful as the day, light, cheerful, and eager to kayak the Roaring Twenties. When I read the description in the guidebooks, this was the day I was most looking forward to. We quickly came up on the first rapid and after some brief directions set off. This was just super fun, huge waves in never ending wave trains for ten miles. Quite a few of my fellow kayakers joined the Colorado River Swim Team that day, but thankfully this was my day to shine. Whenever people ask me about my favorite rapid, it isn't one, but the Roaring Twenties. I was on cloud nine kayaking these rapids and being successful. I also had a "dry hair" run, meaning the kayak never fell over so I didn't have to roll either.

One of our excursions this day was to Redwall Cavern, a large hollowed out cavern to explore. After romping around in there, I realized I was filthy and decided to try to take a "bath" in the river. Once I popped that soap out and started lathering up my hair, I was joined by the other female contingency as we tried to figure out how to stay as clean as possible. The water was still a brisk 48 degrees or so and I have to tell you it felt so good to wash my hair and myself. Group bath in front of the raft guides and men. Yes, we kept our bathing suits on.

By Mile 33 we all hopped onto the rafts and secured our kayaks to run to mile 50 to camp for the night. We wanted to raft through the flat water so we would have more time for hikes and exploring in the higher miles. We camped at a campsite called Dinosaur Camp. This time I set up the cot closer to the water to enjoy the cool water that forms a cool breeze that often blows off the river. I was very unhappy with myself that my feelings of anxiety returned. Sometimes, it is the unknown and new situations that can cause this panic. It isn't the situation itself, just the newness of it. I still could not get my cot up alone and enlisted the help of Rudy (It actually took till four nights to get that thing up alone). With camp set up I went to join the others.

We gathered at night in what became known as the "circle of friends". We would put the camp chairs in a circle and swap stories, visit, drink a cold beverage, and enjoy each other's company. Lola would sketch different scenes from our campsites every night and we eagerly looked forward to seeing the beautiful pictures that came alive off her sketchpad. Tom, a geologist, told us about the rocks and geology and geographical history of the canyon. I am normally a very chatty person but I found on many nights, I just liked to sit in silence and take everything in, the laugher, sounds of the river, cooking sounds, and low conversations. There is a lot to be gained from sitting in silence and listening to others.

After another incredible dinner and our second amusing camp talk by Dave, we headed to bed again at the late hour of 8:30. Once again I lay down on the cot filled with anxiety. But tonight it passed immediately as I lay there and looked at the stars, which tonight seemed like old friends who came to stay by me and comfort me. Their sparkle and light soothed me and I went to sleep feeling like I was in the embrace and under the watchful eyes of dear old friends.

Chapter 11

Kayaking 2007

My mountain bike club decided to go mountain biking at the Ocoee Whitewater Center one day and then go down the Ocoee River in a raft. I had never seen a whitewater river, growing up in Florida I was used to oceans and flat-water rivers. After a day of biking we got into groups of six, received some instructions from the raft guides, and then carried our rafts down to the put-in. As we were walking down I noticed people carrying brightly colored plastic boats on their shoulders. What were those things? When they put them down, I saw they were kayaks. I had vaguely heard of whitewater kayaking, but had never seen it. They were sitting in these tiny little boats with something around their waist holding them in the boat. I thought they were crazy. I remember saying to my friends, "That is nuts. I would never do that." Well fate has a way of making you eat your words. I had the most awesome time on the river rafting. My friend Gail noticed my intense love of water and suggested I give kayaking a try. She whitewater kayaked and said there was an easier river called the Hiawassee. So later that week I found an outfitter online, drove over, and bought the entire set up and drove home with a kayak, and no clue that it actually took skill to paddle it. Apparently, as I was to find out, it does take some skill to whitewater kayak.

Two weeks later, I showed up at the Hiawassee River put in with a Tennessee Valley Canoe Club trip. I must have looked green as can be. Mark, one of the members, targeted in on me and asked if I had ever been in a boat and could I do a wet exit. The stunned look on my face told the answer. So off we went to the river where Mark proceeded to flip me over and over so I could get out of the boat if I flipped over. For those of you who have never sat in a whitewater kayak, you are skirted in and have your thighs beneath hooks that prevent you from falling out if you flip. I was kind of shocked they actually flipped over so easily. After I passed Mark's wet exit test, which is when you demonstrate you can actually get out of the boat if you flip over, we set off and I was hooked. My soul felt at peace paddling down the river even though my heart was pounding with adrenaline and yes a bit of fear. This was also a turning point in my life. Although I loved mountain biking, I wasn't good at it. My asthma and extra weight made it very tough. I could see that I would be good at kayaking and I loved the water. Once again my vet, Mike McGhee, saved the day. He suggested I go to Endless River Adventures to get some kayaking instruction from someone called Juliet, who would help me learn to kayak safely. Another turning point in my life, I had no idea how much Endless River Adventures and the people that work there would become so integrated in my life. I am grateful to Mike McGhee for steering me to a place that I needed to be.

I made an appointment for private instruction and eagerly showed up on a Saturday and met Juliet. I am amazed at how the right people are put in your path in your life when you need them most. I was still struggling with confidence and self-esteem issues. Although it was better, I still could not see myself ever being a strong, confident woman. I still suffered from anxiety frequently and a fear that I would be unable to succeed at things I try. Fifteen years of living in fear of upsetting my husband had taken a toll that even counseling had not been able to totally lick. Juliet was everything I was not. She co-owned her own business, Endless River Adventures, with her husband, Ken. She was strong and confident. She was used to being in a male dominated sport and business, and she handled it well. In the eight years I have known her I have never seen anyone walk all over her. She has been leading kayaking trips to South America for years and teaches many to kayak. She was so confident and sure of herself and her abilities, and I could sense it. "How do you achieve that?" I wondered. We headed off to the lake for stroke and rolling practice then a trip down a small section of the river. I was hooked, this was my sport. I did not have many people to paddle with so only paddled a few times after that, but in 2008 I would paddle much more. Although I didn't know it at the time, Juliet would be the catalyst for many new adventures, meeting lifelong friends, and a social networking group that would give me much happiness over the years. The day I met her my life took a dramatic and unpredictable positive turn in my life and I am thankful to Mike for putting Juliet and the entire Endless River Adventure family into my life.

Chapter 12

Grand Canyon Day 3: Mile 50-75

Rivers are places that renew our spirit, connect us with our past, and link us directly with the flow and rhythm of the natural world.
— Ted Turner, *The Rivers of South Carolina*

Day 3 was the respite before the storm. It was one of those perfect days when you are so thankful to be where you are and in your favorite place, your kayak. I gave my Diesel an affectionate pat on the bow before starting off. I knew the bigger rapids started at mile 75 and today would be a splashy day. As I paddled down the Colorado River in super exciting wave trains, I was feeling confident about running the bigger rapids that lay ahead. I was enjoying the larger features and figuring out the swirly water. I was beginning to be in harmony with the moving water instead of constantly fighting against it. When I fought the whirlpools and swirls and struggled to go in a straight path downstream it exhausted me. Instead of trying to understand the river, follow the path of least resistance, and dance with the water, I was fighting it. When I saw the swirly paths in the water and started to use them, paddling became easier. It might have been a longer route riding the swirls, but it was the calmer path and I got to my desired location more peacefully and easily. Kind of like life, sometimes the better path is to follow the flows, ebbs, and skirt the edges of the turbulence to find the peace and calm we need.

Most people are aware that although the Colorado River appears wild and free, it is a dammed river, meaning the water flow is managed and controlled. The flows at the time I was on it were between 12,000 cfs and 18,000 cfs, depending on how far you were from the dam. The pattern looked like a wave when looking at the graph of the flow. Dave, having paddled the canyon many times, knew exactly when the high water would get to what mile. He was eager to hit the big rapids that started in the 70's at high flow, hence our camp at mile 75. By mile 61, the Little Colorado River had joined in with the Colorado River and soon after the blue/green Colorado had turned into the Big Muddy as it is often called. The water was the color of chocolate milk and thick with silt. I had seen in books that sometimes the Colorado River can be up to 30% silt and it wouldn't surprise me if this were one of those times. That night we did the normal wash up in the river, but with so much silt, more dirt just went on. By this time I was used to being covered in sand and way dirtier then I was used to, but it felt great. It was the kind of dirt that you earned, "the playing hard" and "living large" kind of dirt. I would imagine that some people would find this difficult to live with, but sometimes accepting a situation and just living with it makes life so much easier, and things you thought you might not like are actually quite pleasant. The canyon was accepting me by covering me with its silt and the very essence of the Colorado. I stopped even trying to get my feet sand free before jumping into bed. With the wind whipping the sand around, it would end up there anyway. It became a joke about how much sand we were ingesting. As dinner was being cooked and we were sitting there with our cups drinking, the sand, moved by the wind, would spray us like a sandblaster covering the food, us, drinks and all our belongings with a layer of that fine sand. Eyes were the big problem and I felt awful for those people who wore contacts. I have never been happier and I still miss those nights sitting there getting sand blasted in one of the most beautiful places on earth. Don't sweat the small stuff. Don't complain about things that you can't change. Live in the moment and relish the beauty around you.

Our trip talk that night started as usual, "circle of friends", good food, and Dave standing up with his usual piece of discarded cardboard reading his notes about the next day's adventure. He started off with the rapid Hance at mile 77, the first big rapid we would run. The rapids on the canyon have a unique rating system and Hance is listed as a 7-9, with 10 being the biggest. We would scout it first and decide if we wanted to run it or not. Hance he said, was a fairly easy move, but if you did not get river left fast enough, then you would end up in The Land of Giants. This would result in an enormous beat down where you would get churned under the huge waves and spat at the bottom like a piece of driftwood. His description of the rapid did not exactly inspire me to want to run it. I didn't know it at the time, but Hance would be the start of a very difficult lesson for me, one that took me two days to learn and accept and still was a painful lesson.

Chapter 13

2008

January started off with a phone call from my sister Leslie. Our sister, Dianne, had not shown up for work in Texas and when the police were sent they had found her dead in her bathroom. An autopsy would later reveal that she had a blood clot that killed her before she even hit the floor at the young age of 53. I called in on bereavement leave and headed to Florida to be with my mother, while my sister Leslie, her husband Bill, my sister Karen, and my brother, John, went to Texas to handle things. I will never forget the sight of my mother when I got there. She had aged ten years since I had seen her at Christmas. Dianne had listed my mother as her emergency contact so when the Texas police contacted the Tavares Police Department, they had shown up on my mother's porch asking her questions about Dianne, and she was alone when she was told. My mother was 74 at the time and not in great health. To this day I don't know how she didn't have a heart attack. She looked so lost and sad standing there, tears running down her face, as I got out of my truck and ran into her arms. She reached out to me and hugged me tightly and my heart broke. How could I comfort her? She had just lost her eldest child. We had always been a tight, close knit family. I remembered all those times my mother had held me when I was sad or hurt and all I could do was hold her and hope she knew how much all of her kids loved her. My mother lost a piece of herself when Dianne died, and she was never able to fully recover from the loss.

Although I was faced with overwhelming grief myself, it didn't even come close to the grief my mother felt losing her eldest child. We spent the week together playing games, talking, sharing memories and going to her favorite bar at night. She enjoyed talking with her friends there and watching Nascar races. Friends are very important in your life and I wanted her to be surrounded by hers. I felt like our roles were reversed and I was the parent comforting her and did everything in my power to ease her grief in any way I could. I just did not know what I could do to ease her overwhelming pain when I was faced with such pain myself.

My siblings came back with Dianne's belongings; her ex-boyfriend had taken her dog so we weren't faced with that decision about what to do with the dog. It is not an easy task to sort through a loved one's belongings. So many memories are there, so much that had clearly meant something to her, but to us the meaning was unclear. You feel like a trespasser going through their belongings and giving things away. It's heartbreaking.

My sister's life had been reduced to memories and a few items left that had been brought back. Her belongings were split up, we all took things that had memories for us. We spent a few days together sharing memories. My family does not do funerals well. After my father's a few years before, we decided no more. So we went off to the bar and had a party in my sister's memory. We laughed over her blue bunny PJ's she used to run around in, her uncanny timing showing up just when dinner was served, and how we used to give her pink flamingos as a gag gift constantly. We remembered how she loved pistachio nuts and great meals. We spent the night laughing and sharing our memories of her. We chose to remember my wonderful, funny, caring, sister Dianne with the happiness that she gave us in her lifetime while sharing cold beers. What better tribute can there be?

It was hard for me to return home and leave my mother. She stood there with tears in her eyes as I pulled away. I cried all the way to the Georgia border. I remember calling my friend Debbie Garner, and just bawling on the phone. She must have stayed with me for quite some time as my heart broke again. I started calling my mother every day, part for her and part for me. Hearing her cheered me up and now she was beginning to have a fear of losing her remaining children. It calmed her to hear my voice. My mother's 75th birthday was coming up in June and we had been planning a huge party for her. All of us had planned to attend. Dianne had forgone on coming home at Christmas time so she would have off for the party. I was driving home from work in May and my phone rang. It was my sister, Leslie. She told me to pull over so we could talk about Mom's party. I pulled into a Cracker Barrel Restaurant parking lot. Leslie told me Karen had not shown up for work that morning. I could feel my heart rate go up. They sent the police and found her dead in her bedroom. I kept screaming at my sister to stop kidding me like that. How could we lose two sisters in four months? How could this be happening? It took her a good ten minutes to convince me it wasn't a sick joke.

I called my friend, Jessica, to come and get me. There was no way I could safely drive, I was crying uncontrollably. I sat in my truck and cried. It was pouring and I felt like the world was crying with me as I watched the rain slide down the windows. I called my mother through my tears and told her I would be there tomorrow. I called in to work and told them I would be missing a week of school again and my friends, Bridget Conway and Bridget Davis, told me they would take care of my lesson plans and to just go. I saw a green Isuzu pull up and I thought it was Jessica's and I saw her daughter sitting in the back. I leaped out of my truck and ran into the passenger seat crying. Then I looked up and realized this was not Jessica's car and the women driving was reaching into the backseat to protect her child from this maniac who just leaped in crying. Apologizing I got back out into the rain and saw another green Isuzu pull up. When Jessica came to get me I was a wreck. My husband, and now two sisters dead in two years. I was unable to cope. I cried the entire night and had a friend go and get my truck for me. I packed with a heavy heart and wondered how I could ever stand to see that look on my mother's face gain.

The drive to Florida from Atlanta is not a pretty drive, long, straight and boring and with lots of billboards, nothing to occupy a racing, grief stricken mind. My mother called me every hour checking on my safety. She was now convinced something would happen to me. That eight-hour drive was one of the longest drives I've ever taken. How could I face my mother? My last sister? My brother? Leslie, Dianne, Karen, and John were all close in age; only five years separated the oldest and youngest. I was ten years younger than the youngest, Leslie. We were all close, but the three oldest sisters, being so close in age, had shared a special bond. I saw Leslie and broke down. I felt like my huge family had been so reduced. How would we get by? How did the four Owens/Leatherbury girls get down to just two? I felt lonely and alone. I have never understood how only children can survive in this world so alone. The bonds I have with my siblings are like no other. I always felt so close to them. It is an indescribable love and bond. It is hard to describe the feeling of coming from a large family to someone who doesn't come from one. I am about the 65th grandchild on my mother's side. She was the eighth of fifteen children and they all had a bunch of kids. So I grew up surrounded by this blanket of family that made me always feel so loved and comfortable. The last two years had shaken this feeling.

I pulled into my mother's house and saw my family. We all cried and had long talks sharing memories. Karen had lived twenty minutes from my mother and Leslie and I headed over to clean her house and once again go through a sister's belongings. We cleaned everything up spotless so Mom could get the deposit back, took things to Goodwill, called nieces and nephews to see who needed furniture and brought things of monetary and sentimental value back to Mom's house for us to sort. As we went through Karen's things, it occurred to me how worthless stuff is. She spent time collecting things as we all do, when in reality people are what are really important. This created a shift in my mindset that has become permanent in the upcoming months and remains with me to this day. I sold off everything I had that wasn't needed and I put my 3000 sq foot house up for sale. I had come to the conclusion that "things and stuff" just complicated your life and certainly did not bring happiness. I never once heard any family member lament on the loss of my sisters' things. It was them that we missed and loved, not their belongings. I have been near many terminal people in my life and not one of them wished for more things. Time, family, and love are what they wanted. When faced with the end of your life or someone else's, you realize that time spent with your family and friends are all that matters.

Once again we headed back to the bar and toasted the life of another lost sister. We spoke of the good times, trip to Disney World, games we had played, and her love of Sudoku puzzles. Funerals to me focus on the death and the loss. We chose to focus on the life she lived and the love we had for her. We spent the week as a family and then with a heavy heart I drove home. That drive home really hit me. How could I cope losing two sisters so close? And worse, how could my mother ever survive this? I was still not recovered from living without my husband and making choices alone. Now the void created by Dianne and Karen's deaths seemed impossible to fill. I had had nightmares after Jim died. Some involved him not breathing and my not being able to hook up the oxygen, others were him upset with me, and some were vague. The most vivid recurring dream I have of Jim is the doctors tell me he is still alive and when Jim sees me he tells me I can't kayak or be with my friends any more. I wake up in a cold sweat. Now those nightmares started again along with ones where I'd lose other family members. When you lose that many people in such a short time, you worry how many more will you lose? It got so bad that whenever my sister called at some odd time, she started off with "everyone is OK." I had signed up for a Tennessee Valley Canoe Club (TVCC) paddle school after Memorial Day and I felt that maybe whitewater kayaking might be a way for me to have fun, enjoy the outdoors, and help with the grief. You just can't sit around the house crying. You have to get out and enjoy life.

After paddle school I was hooked. I now had people to paddle with and found myself in a boat on most weekends. I continued to take classes with Endless River Adventures with Juliet and Steve, another instructor. My skills improved and I found joy. The people that you paddle with are so supportive and unlike most sports you don't compete against others and I needed that support. I started to feel that I could do things well, that I could succeed at something. Juliet thought that I would like a class 2/3 Costa Rica kayaking trip in November. I hadn't traveled internationally since I went to

Europe with my father when I was 16. I quickly ordered my first passport since I was a teen. The kayaking didn't start until Sunday so I took two days off work and made some plans to see Costa Rica. I wanted to zip line, do some hikes, and see a volcano and some wildlife. This would entail my traveling alone in a foreign country and I did not speak one word of Spanish at the time. I found a place in La Fortuna that sounded great and a tour company that did all the things I wanted. I booked the plane ticket, hotel, and tours. I found a semi-private transportation company and booked a trip from San Jose to La Fortuna and back again. I felt a sense of pride that I had done these things myself.

When the time came to board the plane I was scared to death. My husband had died just two and a half years ago and now I was flying to a foreign country alone. It was hard to believe just a short time ago I had never been to the grocery store by myself and never made my own decisions or even filled up a gas tank. The plane landed in San Jose and I nervously cleared customs, carrying my kayak gear and suitcase. I hailed a cab with a driver who amazingly spoke some English and went to a hotel. I was scared to death, literally shaking. This seemed like a much better idea when I was sitting on the couch alone and reading the Lonely Planet Costa Rica Book. Latin American countries are very loud, resembling a Fourth of July party or some kind of coup. It is sometimes hard to tell. This partying, music, fireworks, goes on all night. My room was outside in a foyer with a very flimsy door lock. I crawled under the covers too full of fear, excitement, apprehension, and anticipation to slow my racing thoughts and get to sleep. A tiny kitten was outside my room meowing and against my better judgment I invited it in. It quickly jumped onto my bed and it purred me to sleep. Breakfast came with the room and I had my first taste of Gallo Pinto, an incredible rice and bean dish typical in Costa Rica, and the freshest fruit I have ever had. The hotel helped me get a cab to the shuttle and off I went to La Fortuna, alone in Costa Rica. This is when I discovered there were only traffic suggestions, not laws in Costa Rica. It was like being in a Nascar race with potholes, bikes, pedestrians, and a myriad of vehicles everywhere. I could not believe I made it to La Fortuna in one piece.

My hotel was located right in the center of the city of La Fortuna and I spent the afternoon exploring. People that know me know how much I like to talk. It was killing me that I couldn't speak to anyone. I have since made an attempt to learn Spanish, one of the best things I have done. I felt my fear melt away as the friendliness of the Costa Rican people washed over me. They didn't care that I didn't speak Spanish, only a few words. They told me new Spanish words, tried to talk to me, and helped me out when I was lost. I enjoyed shopping, eating ice cream, and a wonderful dinner in the typical outside restaurants so common in Latin America. I think most Latin Americans feel like I do, that being outside is just good for your soul. I enjoyed the fresh air and liveliness of this Latin American country. Latin American cities have a color and richness to them that is unique. The happiness and party type atmosphere is contagious and you can't help but smile. I am used to dead bolts and the only lock on the door was one of those tiny ones in the door handle. At this point I decided to myself "When in Rome, do as the Romans do". I dropped all my preconceptions of what a city should be and enjoyed it for what it was. I slept very deeply among the mariachi music, car horns honking, and the sounds of people laughing and shouting.

Next morning was zip-lining. I was picked up at the hotel by the tour operator and joined a mix of people from Europe and North America for the trip. This is when I first figured out travelling alone is a wonderful thing. It forces you to meet other people, people that you might not get to know otherwise and to experience the local culture. I find now that I often enjoy travelling alone as much as being in a group. I enjoyed learning about everyone on our trip and felt that I was among new friends. I couldn't believe that I had planned this, got on a plane by myself, flew internationally and was having the time of my life on a solo trip. The zip lining was incredible. One of the cables was over 1/4 mile long adjacent by an active volcano through dense rain forest. As I was whizzing along, I realized I was an adventure traveler and would be for life. That night we went to see the Arneal Volcano with a different group of people. We watched hot lava balls roll down the side of the mountain under a star filled sky in the middle of a rain forest. It was incredible.

The next day was canyoneering. I am a bit klutzy and was concerned to be rappelling down waterfalls in the middle of a jungle. There was only one other couple on my tour. We were fit into harnesses and had a short practice plunge on how to brake yourself while descending. This was not Disney World. You were in control of your own descent and speed. We first went down a ten-foot waterfall. I got the hang of pushing off and releasing the brake at the same time while being cascaded in a spray of water coming off the drop. I did end up head first one time, hanging in my harness, perplexed as to how to get upright again and had to walk myself into position and start again. This trip consisted of over ten rappels, some down waterfalls and some free-falls off platforms. The entire time you are in the middle of a rainforest and enjoying the most beautiful scenery ever. The last rappel was a 125 foot free fall off a platform next to a waterfall. By now I had the braking down. There was someone on the bottom holding the cable and could hold it tight to slow you down if you failed to brake. I walked out on the platform, turned around, leaned back so just the tips of my toes were on the platform and I was now parallel to the ground and pushed off and released. I was sliding down right by the waterfall at a very fast pace. The spray from the waterfall fell around me as I accelerated down the rope. I slowed down and braked with a perfect landing. What an incredible adrenaline rush that was. I had just rappelled and I felt so alive afterwards.

The last day was a hike on a hanging bridge tour, we saw Coati, more birds than I can count, an eyelash palm pit viper in a tree, monkeys, and a sloth. The guide was a young Costa Rican whose English was very good. He made a point of showing and explaining to us the incredible ecosystem we were in.

After the tour, I boarded the transport with an older man and a woman I was sure was his prostitute and found they were actually interesting to talk to as we headed back to San Jose and met up with Juliet, Ken, and the ERA crew. The rains had been severe and the rivers were flooded so we headed to the beach to do some kayak surfing! Jaco Beach was incredible. We had suites right across from the beach. There were hammocks, a pool, and incredible food. We dropped our stuff and hit the beach. I grew up in the Ocean and although I have always been somewhat of a chicken, the last few days had increased my confidence. However when I saw those huge towering waves and I was supposed to paddle out and catch them to surf them in my kayak, I thought they were crazy. I tried once, flipped, swam in and landed by Ken's feet. I told him in no uncertain terms that I was not getting back out into that water. He looked me square in the eye and said in the voice only Ken can master, "You have 60 seconds to get yourself together, get back in the boat, and you are getting back in the water." He literally drug me out there and held the boat in waist deep water until I knew how to correctly lean into the waves. Then he directed me out into the big ones. I caught one and rode it in and flipped. At this point I had never had a successful roll in an accidental flip situation, which we call a combat roll. I rolled it up in the surf for my first ever combat roll. I was so excited. Kayak surfing became one of my favorite things. Sometimes you make the wrong choice about quitting on something and you might need the strong voice of a friend to help you make the right choice and succeed.

The high water made kayaking somewhat of a challenge and there were days when the rivers were just too high, but we had great sightseeing trips and loads of fun. The days we did kayak were thrilling and exciting. At one point I paddled under a branch hanging over the river and looked up to see a huge iguana sunning itself and toucans in the trees. This was the first of many trips down south with ERA. I go to Costa Rica or Ecuador every year with them now.

While many things helped me on my road to recovery, this trip was for sure a catalyst for a change in my life. I had gone from never going anywhere alone to travelling internationally solo and having the time of my life. I often hear people say they want to travel, but don't have anyone to go with. Go alone! Have an adventure! Meet new people and experience different cultures.

I have some rules when travelling internationally. I never eat at an American restaurant. I purposely pick restaurants with no "gringos" in them. I support the local business and experience the food and enjoy the culture. At no point do I ever say or even think things like "In America we do this..." So you can't put toilet paper in the toilet, it's just different, not worse, not a big deal. So some of the showerheads have live electrical wires to heat it, don't stick your hands up high. Pedestrians never have the right of way in a Latin American country. These things are just different and if you constantly try to compare them to what you are used to you will fail to see the beauty and richness of the place where you are. Forget your watch or at least worrying about a time frame. Some cultures have a different definition of "on time". Mas o menos was one of the first terms I learned in Spanish. 8:00 mas o menos. If you are there on time and no one else is, take a walk, talk to people, and stop to smell the roses. The best rule is don't avoid the locals, embrace them, talk to them, and visit with the waitress, the clerk, the hotel clerk, the cab driver. I have had some of my best conversations ever with cab drivers. They also can understand the worst Spanish ever. I have had quite a few personal city tours with cab drivers that were probably better than a licensed tour operator. These cities are theirs and they know them well. I once was having trouble with the currency in Costa Rica and a nice shop owner took lots of cash out of her drawer and made sure I knew the larger numbers. There are 500 colones in a dollar so some exchanges could use large Spanish numbers. She spent thirty minutes with me using the cash from her register to make sure I could count my own change and understood.

I closed off 2008 with a Christmas visit to my mother. I knew this Christmas would be especially tough on all of us. It was just Mom and me for Christmas Eve. Christmas in my family had always been huge with many relatives, presents, food, and happiness. That was the year that I decided Christmas was just too painful for me to deal with any more and I think my mother agreed. The bar she visited was having a Christmas Eve party so we went there and spent the evening with her friends. Christmas at a bar was certainly a different way to celebrate Christmas, but different was a good thing. I was remembering my father taking such care to wrap presents, fights with wrapping paper rolls, the laughter, huge families, and I just don't think I could have taken a Christmas without my sisters, father, and the loneliness that would have ensued.

My mother and I had beer, ate Turduckin, side dishes and there was laughter and happiness among her friends. Sometimes when your life changes things so dramatically, you try to recapture what was lost and it just isn't possible. So a different type of celebration was what was needed. My sister and her husband came by on Christmas day, as well as my brother, for present exchange and dinner on Christmas night. After everyone left, I was curled up in my mother's bed and watching TV with her. She had COPD and her health had been deteriorating for years. This Christmas was hard on her and we were in bed by 7:00. You know when you are little and you ask your parents a question about a serious or painful topic for which there really is no answer? My mother looked at me with an expression like a five year old and said, "Why would God do this to me? I can never forgive him for taking my two girls from me." I had no answer for her and my heart broke. She looked like a small child, so fragile, so lost. I just held her as she cried. I have experienced loss, a husband, father, grandmothers, sisters, but nothing can compare to losing your own child, and I can't imagine how she ever survived losing two.

Chapter 14

Day 4: Miles 75 to 95

"The river is constantly turning and bending and you never know where it's going to go and where you'll wind up. Following the bend in the river and staying on your own path means that you are on the right track. Don't let anyone deter you from that."
— Eartha Kitt

I feel like this chapter should have a unique name, but the name I would call it changes with the days. If I had written this on the night of day four, the chapter would have been called "The Kayaking day that shall not be mentioned". Now, sitting in my house recalling the events with time lessening the disappointment, maybe "Day of Change" or "Day of Acceptance" might be better. In reality the emotions I felt on this day were so complex, that I am not sure any title other than Day 4(although if this was TV some very ominous music playing as the title was read would be fitting) would do it justice.

The problem with kayaking, as I assume in most sports, is some people are just better than others, and some have a much steeper learning curve. We have fun kayaking, love the sport, and try hard, but being a great kayaker eludes us. Now some people would say I'm an excellent kayaker due to the fact that I keep trying, do learn and progress, albeit slowly, and more importantly am a good ambassador on the river. I spend time helping new people out, always will give someone a lift, pick up trash when I see it, and enjoy kayaking. As kayaking levels go, the skill levels are 1 to 5, so you could be class 2 boater or a class 2/3 boater. I have been a class 3 boater for five years now, those elusive class 4 rapids are often out of my reach. I've run some, but not easily and probably not always as skillfully as I would choose. So I stay at the class 3 and watch everyone progress quicker than me. Most times it doesn't hurt, I'm proud of being persistent and loving the sport, but day four was different.

I wanted so badly to be successful in the Grand Canyon, as I defined success. Now everyone's definition of success varies widely. As with most people, I am very hard on myself. Being stuck at that class 3 level for so many years is very frustrating and disappointing. When I was getting ready to go on the Grand Canyon, I was told all the rapids were straight forward and non-consequential, and should be able to run the hard ones without any problems. I had set these expectations for myself that I would be running Hance, Horn, Granite, Crystal, Hermit, and Lava. I would be kayaking the rapids of legend and emerge victorious or at least emerge swimming, but having run them.

Quite often we set the bar too high and this was the case with me. It was apparent from the moment I saw Hance Rapid that I didn't have the skill to run it safely. I gave myself a 50/50 chance of making it down in the boat. The problem was the "Land of Giants". Those waves and holes looked huge from way up here so I knew that from there they must be humongous. Getting on that raft was one of the most difficult and painful things I have done. To me it was admitting that I was a failure kayaking. All the instruction I took, all those days in the water practicing, and I still could not run a larger rapid. I got on the raft dejected. I was so upset with myself that I couldn't even watch my friends run the rapid. Seeing them be successful was like a knife in an open wound for me. I was happy for them and glad they made the line safely, but their success was just another example of my failure. Some of this I know stems from the verbal abuse I took from my husband and it still after all these years hurts. But when you work so hard for something and you can't achieve it and you realize your best isn't good enough, it just plain hurts. Day 4 was just an awful day for me.

This pattern would repeat itself for Horn and Granite rapids. Horn was just dangerous if you missed the line and as much as it pained me to get in the raft, I wasn't stupid. Way better to be disappointed then hurt. Granite loomed and it was said you couldn't scout it, so I got in the raft in the bathtub section. This is the very front section, which offered the most sensational wet ride you could imagine in a raft. Dom was the boatman whose raft I often ended up in. He had a unique, dry sense of humor that at times was hard to figure out. As Dom dropped the raft over the horizon line and I saw Granite. That rapid was enormous. In the trip talk the night before, Dave described this rapid as mass chaos and chaotic, huge munchy exploding waves everywhere. That didn't even begin to do it justice. We were totally immersed in a maelstrom of waves. As we cleared the rapid and turned the raft around I saw my friends all over that rapid, right-side up, upside down, one swimming and people in every part of it trying to stay in their boat. I made the right choice to stay in the raft, but still.

I had asked Dave if there was one safe big rapid I could try and the answer was Hermit. Hermit Rapid was right above our camp for the night. Safe swim if that should happen, just big waves. "How big?" I asked, "Oh big, Oceanic, not so much exploding, they might be 25 feet high." At this point Matt paddled over and said "Mary, there can't be a 25 foot standing wave on a river, it just isn't possible." As we neared the top of the rapid I could hear it, but as usual not see anything. We were at the high flow, about 18,000 cfs at this point, and Dave wasn't sure how big the 10th wave would be at this level. I had no clue what the 10th wave was, but I was pretty sure I wouldn't be calm enough to count. I saw Dave drop over the horizon line and give me the thumbs up sign. So I entered the same spot he did and looked up to see walls of water. Walls of chocolate brown water. And all this water was moving VERY, VERY fast. I started climbing up the first wave, digging in the blade as hard as I could and reaching over the top of the wave and pull myself over. I felt my stomach lurch as I dropped and still another wave. Then I saw this wave that must have been 25 feet high. Well, Matt you were wrong. I made it up the huge wave which I was sure was the legendary 10th wave, cleared it and dropped over the side and looked up. There is a scene in the movie *The Poseidon Adventure*, where the huge wave is about to topple the ship. That describes the legendary 10th wave which now loomed in front of me. I started up panic stricken and it collapsed on me and I was over. I tried to roll but just couldn't, and I found myself swimming, holding on to my kayak and bobbing down the center of the waves. Craig paddled up to me and said, "You must have had the time of your life before that last wave." I was still a bit apprehensive as I got back in the boat. Camp was not even half a mile downstream and we set up camp.

As the night wore on and we were sitting in our circle, all I could think about was how I was such a horrible paddler. How could everyone else being doing so well when I , who try so hard, was failing miserably. I smiled and laughed along with everyone else, but to be honest all I wanted to do was go home and be away from all these reminders of success and my failure slapping me in the face.

Once again I am drawn to the fact that we are too hard on ourselves. No one else was upset I swam, everyone was supportive and two others swam that rapid as well, but I have struggled with rolling a kayak since I first started. It isn't so much the skill required, but the confidence and belief in the roll is what I lack. I just couldn't stand to be there with everyone laughing and went to bed early. One of the best pieces of advice I had gotten on this trip was from Andrea. "You have to find your own happiness." Don't rely on others or situations, find your own happiness wherever you are. I was determined to do better on the next stretch of water. The huge ones were past for a while, so I was going to kayak more tomorrow. I would get that roll and be successful. I'm not sure about expectations and setting goals. Sometimes they are good, but often they set you up for failure and disappointment. But I really did try to find my own happiness.

Chapter 15

Family

The next year went by with a love of kayaking building. I found that when I kayaked, my grief was gone. I took great pleasure in interacting with my paddling peers from a three state area. I relished in the fact that I had made my own friends and was doing well kayaking. Everyone progresses at their own pace and mine was a bit slower than others, but I was still progressing. Your progress was easy to see kayaking, but it's not linear, some days you paddle better than others. One reason I had difficulty learning to kayak was I still had that nagging fear that I wasn't good enough. I could still hear Jim's voice in my head telling me that. But my friends were always encouraging and supporting me and most days I was very happy. My life was on track again. I knew these things took time and I wasn't dealing just with my husband's death and admitting we had an abusive relationship. I had to deal with Dianne and Karen's death and my mother's declining health.

I was awakened by a ringing phone one March morning very early. I heard my sister crying on the other end. I knew someone had died, but could not get it out of her who. Finally, she told me her ex-husband had been killed in a motorcycle accident. She and Dennis had just grown apart, but they were still the parents of their two adult children and the care between them was still there. I knew my sister would be dealing with her children and their loss on top of the still raw emotions we both had over our sisters' deaths a year before. I could not take time off due to the upcoming state assessment tests, but I talked daily to her and my niece, who was taking it especially hard. It just seemed that our family could not get a break.

I closed the school year and once again the guidance counselors wished me a good summer. I was going to spend time in North Carolina kayaking and Florida with my mother and sister. I had a kayak instruction day planned at ERA in early July and had just reached the store when my cell service kicked in again and I saw my sister's number. I pulled in and parked the car before I took it, knowing it was something bad. I took a deep breath and heard my sister crying again. Mom had passed out and the paramedics had rushed her to the hospital. It was not looking good. I rushed in to tell Ken to tell Juliet that I would not be there today and what had happened. I am still not sure exactly what I told him through my tears, but I did sit there a minute and get myself together before I drove home. By then it was too late to leave for Florida, I packed the car, got a pet sitter, unpacked my kayak stuff and tried to get some sleep. I left around 3:00 am.

My sister greeted me at the door in tears. If Mom pulled through this she could no longer live alone. I knew that would upset her deeply, she loved her house. After my father died, she had it built specially for her and moved there. Mom was in bad shape and they were trying to stabilize her. Leslie had to go back to Jacksonville and get the house ready for Mom to live there. I was going to stay there with Mom during the day and start packing up her house at night. I am not sure what is harder, going through things when someone is alive or dead. I saw every little memory she had kept and loved, her plates, kitchenware, cardinal collection, lawn ornamentals, and her furniture. She loved it all and it fell to Leslie, her husband, Bill, and me to figure out what to do with it.

I got to the hospital and was greeted at the desk by nurses asking about DNR (do not resuscitate orders) and Living Wills. I was the youngest child, how did I get in charge? I called Leslie who had these papers and then went in to see Mom. It is so hard to see loved ones like that. I remembered the excellent care that I had as a child from Mom and knew we would have to repay it now. She looked so vulnerable. She cried when she saw me and struggled to get her breath. I held her hand and talked to her for hours during the day until they ran me out. She was so afraid to be alone. My mother, however, still had her wicked sense of humor. She flirted with the male nurse that came to take care of her and asked me to smuggle in a cigarette and Busch beer for her.

I went back to her empty house and cried. COPD is an awful disease that slowly robs one of one of the ability to breathe. It becomes so laborious to breathe that you keep losing weight from burning the calories you expend trying to pull in air. She was already down to about 85 pounds. I knew my sister, brother, and I had a long road ahead of us. The emotional toll of taking care of someone terminal is very difficult, one of the hardest things I have ever done. I started boxing up my mother's house and contacting nieces, nephews, and aunts, to see who wanted Mom's furniture and belongings. And again I was sorting through Diane and Karen's belongings that were in Mom's house. We went through mom's clothes and belongings to see what she would need to live at Leslie's house. The hospital said she would need to go into a rehab nursing home before she went to live with Leslie. We called her insurance plan and nursing homes weren't covered. My mom was old enough to be on Medicaid, but she had worked for the VA and had never paid into Social Security. I was sure she had said she had it so we called Medicaid. We gave them her Social Security number and my father's. They had no record of her having Medicaid. I scoured her safe, filing folder, purse, no card. I am not sure what made me think of this, but I knew she received Social Security each month from her first husband. We finally found his social security number on my mom's marriage certificate. Sure enough, she did have Medicaid under him and we had 40 days of nursing home coverage. Leslie and I visited some places and found one that looked great. My father had died in a long-term care facility, and we had promised my mother we would never put her there. She didn't want to go, or move out of her house, or move in with my sister, but she had no choice. Leslie, John, and I had become the parents. We got my mother secured in the nursing home and I went home.

The rest of the year was spent running back and forth to Florida on every break I had. Mom moved in with Leslie and her husband, Bill. Mentally she was sharp as could be. She did crossword puzzles every morning, read books, and had engaging conversations. We decided that we would let her eat what she wanted, drink what she chose, smoke if she wanted. Nothing she did at this point made a difference. We wanted her to be happy. When I came to visit, she asked that I pull my air mattress on the floor in her room and we had sleep over parties. She was in bed by 6:30 or 7:00. We lay in there and watched Cupcake Wars, Chopped, and other similar shows that made her smile. We giggled like school kids. One of our nightly rituals was to eat this little cup of vanilla ice cream. My sister has a dachshund, Elbe, which my mother absolutely loved. Elbe was not supposed to get people food. My mother was sitting on her bed eating that ice cream with the dog next to her. I looked up and she was giving a spoonful to the dog and one to her. My mother, who was so careful to clean things, is eating after a dog with the biggest smile on her face. I had to laugh. She was happy with her grandpuppy, Elbe. This went on every night until one night I looked up and saw Leslie watching. I starting pssting to my mom to let her know she was in trouble. Mom looked up at Leslie while the dog was licking her spoon, then looked back down at Elbe and said, "Busted". This caused us all to go into uncontrollable laughter. It was like a sleep over with friends, and I am so thankful we spent that time together.

When mornings came, Mom and I had a ritual. We found the two crossword puzzles in the newspaper, and a third online and made two copies of each. While we ate breakfast we worked to solve them, each on the same one. We helped each other, but had some friendly competition too. We did all three puzzles that way. Those months with my mother were moments I will cherish. We were so close and Mom was more like a child then, playing and laughing and kidding around often. I was learning to roll my kayak on the left side, sometimes referred to as an off side roll. Although the thought of me upside down in a kayak must have scared my water-phobic mother, she always helped me. She would sit outside in her chair smoking and watching me in the pool. I told her where my head and arms should be and had her watch me. She knew nothing about kayaks, but she loved to help me. By the end of a week doing about two hours a day, I had a great left roll! It was those little things that made memories. I visited again for Thanksgiving break, but something was weighing heavily on me.

For my Christmas break, I had bought plane tickets to Ecuador and booked a Galapagos trip and a week kayaking, my dream trip. I had a long talk with Mom and she told me I should go. Her feelings were that I was always there for her and this one time really didn't diminish how much I loved her. We had had a close relationship our whole lives. Christmas was still hard on both of us and I knew this would probably be her last Christmas. We had a wonderful Thanksgiving week together and shared many happy memories.

The brightest spot in this time for our family was that my niece, Shelly, Leslie's oldest child, was expecting her first child. Leslie was beyond excited that she was going to be a Grandma. My mother's last dream was to make it to see that baby born. The due date was mid-February, 2010. Mom was doing well when I left her at Thanksgiving and we were hopeful that she would make the birth of Shelly's child. I bought a phone card so I could call Mom daily from Ecuador and had my cell phone as a backup. I really wasn't concerned how much it would cost. I still felt guilty about going to Ecuador over Christmas, but Mom was right. We have always shared a special, loving bond.

Chapter 16

Grand Canyon Day 5: Miles 95 to 110

There are many ways to salvation, and one of them is to follow a river.
— David Brower, Foreword to *Oregon Rivers*
by Larry Olson and John Daniel

It's funny how I am writing this after the trip and how differently I perceive things that happened and wonder how they really happened. Day 5 was not a great day kayaking for many reasons, but it was in other ways. In retrospect it wasn't as bad as I thought, but then what is?

I had trepidations about kayaking after the Hermit incident, but got back in. I knew Crystal was at mile 99 and I had read too much about that to run it. I know the horror stories involve rafts, but still I couldn't get myself to tackle that rapid. I was the only one that pulled out above it and rafted it down. I opted to stay on the raft for the next two rapids and put in below them. We were coming up on the jewel rapids, Sapphire was the first named rapid and of course I swam it. I just gave up. I got in the raft and did not paddle the rest of the day. So I paddled maybe three miles that day.

We got out to hike at Elves Chasm. I hate walking over rocks, steep drop offs and crazy hiking. I had not set any expectations for myself about hiking. I would do what I could do and nothing more. Rob and Chris were determined to get me to this magical, beautiful place. It wasn't a bad hike but some places were narrow and both of them stayed with me till I got to the chasm. It was so worth it, a beautiful pool of water with a waterfall cascading over green moss. It almost looked too pretty to be real as if someone had designed this perfect, magical place. People were swimming under the waterfall and scrambling up the rocks to jump off the ledge into the pool, maybe an eight-foot drop. Considering the state I was in from kayaking failure, it was amazing that I got up there when everyone thought I couldn't. I have a tear in my rotator cuff and pushing up my weight and climbing is not easy for me. Soon I was up with a little rock scrambling and heard cheers as I leaped off the ledge into the pool. As cautious as I am I had never leaped off anything like that. I felt a tremendous sense of accomplishment swimming in the almost magical pool.

We were camping a mile down at a place called The Big Dune, and that's what it was, a Big Dune. Tomorrow would be the halfway point and I was so disappointed in myself. How could I keep swimming when I had such a good roll? It made no sense at all. By now, I was so nervous about swimming and failing that I could barely kayak at all. Every wave threw me off and scared me. I had to figure out what I was going to do. I knew there were big hikes planned on day six and it would be a short kayaking day. I decided no kayaking, no hiking for me. I needed to reset my adrenalin, expectations, mindset, whatever, or this was going to be a long awful six days. I was going to find my happiness and this was the day. Sometimes you just have to step back so you aren't constantly hit with unending failure. I had spent a lot of money on this trip and I was surrounded by the best people you could imagine in one of the most spectacular places on earth. No way was I going to spend this trip miserable. I was going to find my own happiness and the first step was to stop being so hard on myself.

Day 6 could be called rejuvenating day. The day I rested my body, soul, and decided to be a bit nicer to myself.

Chapter 17

Ecuador Trip

Mom was doing well when I boarded the plane to head for Ecuador. I spoke with her from the airport and said goodbye. I was looking forward to my first trip to Ecuador but had some trepidations. I had learned a few words and phrases in Spanish and how to conjugate verbs and I had a translation dictionary, but English was rare to non-existent in Ecuador. I was going to land in Quito and be picked up by Angel, friend and driver for Ken and Juliet, to be taken to the hotel. Travelling in Ecuador is not the same as travelling in Costa Rica. Costa Rica is tourist friendly, you can drink the tap water and they speak English often. Ecuador is the opposite of that. It's a very friendly country with friendly people, but the chance of finding someone who speaks English is rare. Ecuador is adventure travel for sure. Even Quito is an experience that should not be missed. It is exotic, busy, and all in Spanish, full of centuries old rich culture. I was more apprehensive about this trip than the Costa Rica trip. Angel was going to take me to Otovalo, a huge outdoor market, on Saturday, then to the airport Sunday morning for my flight to the Galapagos. I think Ken was worried about me since they left me their driver. My plane couldn't land in Quito due to overcast skies and we were diverted to Guayaquil. By the time we landed in Quito it was 3:30 am, four hours past my flight time. I felt sure Angel would have left and I was prepared to take a cab. I should have known better. I got off the plane and saw a sign that said "Mary Mills" on it with a smiling Angel. I had no idea what an awesome friend Angel and his wife Katy, would become to me over the years.

I was exhausted so he drove me to the hotel and walked me up to my room and locked me in. He really only speaks Spanish and we were muttering through, but he said, "Ken says take care of you," and that he did. He was there at eight the next morning and drove me in his car to Otovalo. We stopped and ate odd fruit along the side of the road, took side trips to see llamas and scenic views, and just had a great time. Even though the language barrier was an issue, I felt like I had known him forever. He walked everywhere with me and helped me haggle with the vendors. He carried my bags, helped me find good deals, and told me about his beloved Ecuador. I was amazed at how much I understood and how quickly my Spanish improved. I fell in love with Ecuador that day. On the way back to the hotel, my exhaustion hit me. I just could not stay awake. I feel asleep in the car listening to Salsa music. Once again, Angel escorted me up to my room, carried my bags in, told me he would be there at 6:00 am to take me to the airport and made sure the door was locked behind me.

I repacked, stored my kayak gear in the storage room, and met Angel downstairs. I was surprised when Angel parked and walked me into the airport. He took me from place to place, paying the Galapagos fee, getting me through customs and security. He sat me down in front of the terminal and told me he would see me in a week and to have fun. He was off to drive Ken and Juliet again. I was finding a new found confidence in myself through solo traveling. It takes some guts to travel around a foreign country where you don't speak the language. I would be flying on Aerogal, an Ecuadorian airline, and find my own way through the Galapagos.

I had been calling my mother daily with the calling cards and she was still doing well. I enjoyed telling her of my adventures. Galapagos would be one of the greatest adventures of all. I was teaching life science at the time and my head was filled with Darwin and the science that I would see there. The airport at the Galapagos was a shock. You walk out across a tarmac. They put your bags out in a row and the drug dogs and produce dogs walk by them sniffing. Then you just walk over and get your bag. I hailed a cab and went to my hotel overlooking the ocean. My cruise ship was leaving the next day, so I had a while to explore the Island. I had a map and set off for the museum at the other end of the Island. This entailed a walk across the beach, normally not a problem, but I had to pass by, over, and through herds of sea lions. I am not entirely sure that you know how big those things are and they honk at you loudly. I just could not get past them even though the little children were giggling at me. Finally some older lady came over grabbed my hand and said, "mismo el perro," which means "like a dog," and pulled me through with a firm grip. I think my fear was evident to her. Some things don't need a common language to understand. I stepped over them and was so close to them, I couldn't believe it. They didn't move as we passed. I thanked the lady and went on my way. The beauty and mystic of this place is indescribable, a wonder at every turn, wildlife, plants, and scenery.

I ate dinner in an open restaurant on the hotel roof, a Darwin Finch actually landed on my table while I was eating. I had a guide book for all the finch varieties on the island and spotted three of them that night. I went for an evening stroll down the boardwalk on the water. The next morning I took a walk and saw an elderly lady sitting on a bench. I got up the nerve and said, "como se dice" and pointed to the sea lion expecting a quick answer. "Lobo del Mar," she answered. Then she motioned me over to the bench. She asked where I was from which thankfully I had practiced, and she then proceeded to give me a noun lesson in Spanish. She was amazed at how little I knew and was doing her best to rectify my lacking Spanish. I must have sat there an hour with my translation dictionary talking to her. That is when I realized it isn't important how bad your pronunciation is or if you mess up a verb. What is important is you try. The locals love to help you with Spanish, and they love to learn English and learn about the States. And once again, had I been travelling in a group, I might have missed the opportunity to meet such a wonderful local person.

I boarded the boat via a water taxi around noon and then the fun began. Ken and Angel had found the perfect ship, with a female roommate, and the best room on the ship, up top! We had ocean views and fresh air. I was the only American on the ship that holds sixteen people. Four Alaskans had missed the connection flight and would try to meet us the next day by speedboat. That week was incredible. I swam with sea lions, penguins, and sea turtles. I saw Blue Footed Boobies, Galapagos Hawks, and Albatrosses. A baby albatross was taking its first flight off the cliff and I watched him take a leap of faith of the cliff and take his first flight ever. I saw lava lizards, tortoises, and so many sea iguanas. The iguanas were the size of small alligators and they had no fear of you whatsoever. People who know me know that I am not a big fan of lizards. We had to step over them and around piles of them and that took some nerve. They have this adaptation to get rid of salt in their bodies; they shoot it out their nostrils and I had to dodge salt sprays while walking through them. It made me wonder if they had contests to see who could hit the most tourists in a day. We swam and snorkeled for hours every afternoon with sharks and over reefs with tons of sea-life. We hiked into a pitch black lava tube, up to the edge of a cliff with spectacular views, and hiked through barren landscapes, lava fields, and grounds that just crawled with iguanas and lava lizards. It was a trip of a lifetime, a spectacular experience.

The food on the ship was incredible. I have no idea how they managed in the kitchen the size of a small closet in a heavily pitching boat. They moved us at night from island to island and the ship tossed so much I could not even walk to the restroom, but had to crawl. Luckily, I had put on ear patches for nausea and took pills at night. I was unaffected, unlike the Europeans who apparently did not have seasick ear patches. I gave some to the sickest fellow passengers.

I am still not sure how this worked, but in the morning if I went up top I had cell service and was able to call my mother every day. The crew said it was bouncing off a satellite and not a cell tower. I didn't care how it worked or if I would get charged for it, the chance to to talk to Mom every day and tell her about the beauties I was seeing was priceless. I never got charged for those calls and never did figure out how I made them but am so thankful for those extra days calling my mom.

After a week of living in paradise and seeing things I thought I would never see I was on an Aerogal plane back to Quito where I took a cab to the hotel and met Ken, Juliet, and the ERA guides for dinner. I was so excited to share my trip, but now we were off for another adventure. We spent a week in Tena, Ecuador, kayaking and sightseeing. In contrast to Costa Rica trip, there was a drought here, but there was still plenty to kayak. Our lodge was situated on a monkey preserve. During meals the monkeys tried to swoop down to get your food. They are quick. For dinner the fish were fresh caught in the pond and steamed whole in a banana leaf with vegetables, with tails, heads, and all. Juliet saw me looking perplexed and helped me debone it. It was beyond delicious. The kayaking was fantastic. I left Ecuador leaving a new friend, Angel, and a country that I had grown to love in just two short weeks.

Chapter 18

Day 6: Grand Canyon Miles 119-132

*Sit by a river. Find peace and meaning in the rhythm
of the lifeblood of the Earth.*
— Anonymous

Sometimes we set our expectations too high and we are harder on ourselves than we should be. I had set the bar high for my paddling and when I couldn't meet those goals, instead of just enjoying one of the most beautiful places on earth for what it was, I tried to shape it to fit my expectations and it just didn't work. I was sad when I should have been ecstatic. In addition I was exhausted. Since we had been paddling 25 miles a day as well as hiking. So I decided this was raft day. I was going to reset my mood, be kind to myself, and just soak in all that the canyon had to offer. We had planned on a hike that day and I knew it would be a tough one with issues for those of us afraid of heights. I decided to be nice to myself. When the others started hiking up, I found a peaceful waterfall right off the river in a secluded slot canyon. It was one of the most beautiful places I have been and I had it all to myself. I brought water and the book *Eat, Pray Love* and found a quiet spot in the shade in the midst of waterfall spray. As hot and dry as it was in the canyon, this felt like natural air conditioning. It was heavenly. I settled in and enjoyed reading about someone else who was finding her way in the world.

I realized while I was reading and enjoying the waterfall how lucky I was to be in the Grand Canyon and that my swims and perceived failure didn't really matter. They really weren't failures at all. I enjoyed watching the way the light played on the rocks as the sun rose higher and higher and the shade shifted. After a few hours, the only shade left was under a small outcropping of rock behind a scrub bush. I wondered as I crawled in how many other people over the years had found shelter in this same spot, the last bit of shade during the hottest part of the day. I could almost imagine some young boys centuries ago, huddling under the ledge after enjoying a cool swim talking about their day. I felt a part of something so old and so special sitting there reading. When the others came down from their hike a few hours later, I felt refreshed and rejuvenated and ready for the second half of our trip. I realized I made the right decision in passing on the hike when Keith told me how hard the hike was and how narrow the trail was.

I decided to stay in the raft since the rest of the paddling was short. We had planned on stopping at Stone Creek Campsite earlier than usual to give everyone a much needed break and rest. The problem with that is the sun. It is near impossible to sit in the shadeless beach campsites in the heat of the day with precious little shelter. Luckily Stone Creek had a slot canyon with a waterfall and shade to rest in. Some people chose to do a longer hike up the canyon and the rest of us enjoyed the shade of a slot canyon until the sun went down beyond the canyon walls and the temperature dropped to a bearable level.

Temperatures and conditions are extreme in the canyon and yet have a beauty and magical quality that is hard to quantify and explain to someone who hasn't witnessed it. When the sun hits you on the beach, it is so hot and dry that you feel that you might melt into the canyon and become one with it, then the sun starts setting over the canyon wall and as the blazing sun leaves the canyon, you almost immediately feel changes. The light is softer, the wind picks up and sometimes blows sand on you like a blaster; but other times the air is so still that you can almost feel the ground breathe a sigh of relief for the respite from the heat and intense brightness. The sand that was once so hot you would burn your bare feet on it becomes soft and warm as you dig your toes into it. As the sun sets farther down and light lessens, the shadows accentuate the rock formations and casts ever changing shadows over the landscape.

I felt that I learned a lesson from the canyon on my day of reflection and rest. Just as the sunlight changes the canyon, the canyon had changed me. I need to embrace the changes that life sometimes unexpectedly throws at me and appreciate them. Sometimes you are the sunlight and affect the surroundings of others, but often you are the rock as the sunlight passes over and scorches you. Things might be different, but that is not always a bad thing. Bad events might impact your life more than you would like, but it isn't the end. How you cope with those bad events can make all the difference between happiness and despair. I went to sleep that night by the river, listening to the sound of the Colorado as it rushed by. I was relaxed and looking forward to kayaking again. If I swam, that's all right too, I was blessed to be able to experience such a magical and spectacular place and I was finally in a mental place where I could realize that.

Chapter 19

Mom

I arrived home from Ecuador exhausted, but invigorated. I had taped science lessons when I was in the Galapagos and shared them with my students. We were expecting an ice storm on Friday and school was cancelled. My phone rang early and it was my sister, Leslie, crying. Mom had taken a serious turn for the worse. We had been working with Hospice and they suggested I come down. The problem was there was ice and snow in Atlanta and that totally shuts the roads down. I called the fire department and they said the roads were impassable. I got lesson plans ready for school, emailed them, packed up, got a pet sitter arranged, and prayed for clear roads in the morning.

My long, sloping driveway was a sheet of ice and the road didn't look much better. The fire department said the highways were clear. I just had to get there. Being from Florida I had no experience driving in these conditions. But I got the truck lined up, dropped it in low gear, kept my foot off the brake, slid down the driveway then all the way down the street to the end of the subdivision. I crept the three miles to the highway and as slow as the truck could go slipping and sliding all the way. The highways were deserted as I headed through Atlanta, though thankfully ice free. I coasted over bridges and overpasses with my foot off the brake in case patches of ice existed. It was another long 7 hour drive down Hwy 75 to Jacksonville.

Arriving at Leslie's house in Jacksonville, Florida, I ran in the door expecting the worst. My beautiful, loving mother was a shell of herself. I had talked to her two days before and she was fine. We had joked and had a wonderful conversation. Now she could barely talk, her eyes were out of focus, and I could tell that the end of her precious life was near. My sister, brother, brother in law, and I had the difficult task of deciding what we were going to do: allow my mother to die in the house like she wanted or move her to the Hospice center. The Hospice nurse arrived and let us know what we could expect. Mom would need constant morphine, she was too weak to even have a bowel movement and would need suppositories, and she would need constant medical care, sheets changed if she didn't or couldn't get up to use the restroom. I had taken care of my husband for ten days, and I knew how hard it was to care for people in their final moments. It is not like it is on TV. It is hard, long, and the most gut-wrenching thing you will ever have to live through. I am not sure most people can actually do it without massive help.

We put Mom to bed at 6:00 and once again my air mattress was on the floor in her room. My mother could talk, but I could tell she was tired. I knelt by her bed the entire night holding her hand drifting in and out of sleep, Occasionally Leslie would spot me and I'd curl up on the floor for an hour or two. Mom would intermittently scream for Karen and Dianne and my father. She wanted to see them, and it seemed to me she was talking to them as her eyes focused on a spot in the corner, as she appeared to be having conversations. She kept pleading with me that she wanted to go to them now. I had no answer for her and my heart broke. She hadn't eaten in days and had consumed little fluid. I knew she was weak and she weighed about 80 pounds by this time. I held her hand and comforted her the best I could. I told her stories about my adventures and we recalled stories from our childhood and family vacations. There were times she was calm and I would see her smile as I talked. My mother had never had a loss of mental faculties during her illness, and she could add up those Yahtzee dice faster than I could. She was still beating me at completing the crossword puzzles in November. But now, Mom would stare at a place on the wall and start having a conversation with a lady that I couldn't see. Her eyes focused on someone beyond my comprehension and she would pause and answer questions and talk to her. I just humored her and joined in. The other thing was the cat. Mother was convinced I had brought a cat. She had an imaginary cat sitting on the foot of her bed and I had to pick it up and put it out at night. Mom and I talked off and on. I often fell asleep kneeling there with my head on the bed for a second night. Leslie came in at times and I would collapse on the air mattress in a restless sleep for an hour or two.

By morning it was painfully clear to us we would not be able to do this without help. My sister and I were already emotionally drained. My brother came and we discussed this with the nurse. The guilt we felt at putting her in Hospice was overwhelming after promising her we would let her die at home. A place was found for her and we went to talk to mother. She preferred to stay at home in her final days but was okay going to Hospice Center. She did have a request. She wanted one more cigarette before she went, so we carried her to the garage and let her have her last cigarette. She was so weak at this point we had to help her lift the cigarette to her mouth. I often tell this to my students when we talk about cigarettes. This alone will tell you how addictive cigarettes are and what control they have over your life. The ambulance arrived and I rode with Mom. Mom flirted like crazy with the two male EMT's in the ambulance. She made me laugh as she tried her best to embarrass the two of them. She also made fun of my sister's driving behind us in the ambulance. She could not see her of course, but still made jokes and had us all laughing. I still feel guilty to this day about putting her in Hospice, even though I knew this would be the best for her and she had remarkable care. We wanted her to be as comfortable as possible and we just couldn't provide it at home. We were in a private room with a cot, which would be my home for as long as Mom was living. I had made a decision I would not leave her side.

The nursing attendant, Shondra, became a part of our family. I will forever be indebted to her, one of the kindest people I have ever met. She treated my mother like she was her own mother, always speaking to her with softness in her voice, and handling her with great care. Mom was still alert at the start, but the increase in

112

morphine was causing her to hallucinate. She was afraid to be alone so I pulled up the chair next to her bed. I put some pillows on her bed and slept on and off with my head next to her arm, holding her hand, waking when she did and snoozing when she did. The invisible cat apparently came with us in the ambulance and my mom talked to it frequently. My sister came the next day and I took my brother's dog for a walk in the park. Dogs are allowed in Hospice and my mother was visited by a different therapy dog daily, as well as John's dog, Toby. Elbe, being somewhat of a biter, was not allowed to visit.

When I came back from my walk, my sister was upset. The doctor, trying to be nice, was saying mom was improving and stabilizing and maybe we could bring her home to die. Now I know she meant it to be comforting, but it had the opposite effect. It sent us into a panic attack, wondering how we were going to take care of her alone in the house. I confronted the doctor and told her she was to talk to me only, and that there would be no more talk of bringing her home. I'm sure she thought I was about ready to snap. I'm normally quite mild mannered and really went off on that doctor. That was the last time I left my mother's room other than for brief walks around the center for the next eight days. My sister and brother were there during the day, and often I would snooze on the cot then. At night I stayed by my mother's side. I didn't want her to be alone or scared. Her hallucinations increased, and her awareness decreased over the course of a few days. There came a point when she stopped moving or responding to us at all. She had no pulse in her extremities and had not had liquid or food for many days. I pushed the morphine button for her constantly. This was taking a toll on us. To watch someone you love take labored breaths, in a coma of sorts, is horrible beyond words. As I type this I have a knot in the pit of my stomach and feel the helplessness I felt then. As with my husband, you just pray for an end to everyone's suffering, which brings on waves of guilt. How could I be praying for my beautiful, kind, and funny mother to die? I still talked to her in the remote case she could still hear us. I started talking to Dad, Dianne, and Karen, hoping if there was any chance they could hear me, they could encourage Mother to come to them.

On the ninth day of this, Shondra came in and said our mother must have a big heart and be stubborn as nails to still be alive. "Yes," we replied, with the first laugh we had had in days. Both things described our strong-willed, kindhearted mother. She called another nurse, a friend of hers, in and asked my sister and me to take a walk. They would give mama a bath, put new sheets on the bed, new clothes, wash her hair, make her feel good and relaxed and pretty. She said she knew these things better than the doctors. Mom would go if she felt better; women like to feel pretty and clean. Leslie and I slipped out to get an ice cream. When we came back thirty minutes later, Mom looked great. She was visibly relaxed and breathing better. She smelled good and just looked more at peace than I'd seen her in days. We held her hand and talked to her. We told Mom how much we were enjoying our ice cream and as we were eating it, she made a labored breath, raspy, shaky, and irregular. I had heard this same sound when Jim finally went. I knew it was close. We both knelt over her bed, kissed her, told her how much we loved her and that it was time to go see Dianne, Karen, and Dad. She took one more breath and was gone, just like that, while we were eating ice cream. It was surreal and almost unbelievable. Somehow it was appropriate that we shared that one last ice cream together. We were so wiped out, exhausted, physically and emotionally drained, there were few tears. We were in shock but relieved that she wasn't suffering.

Shondra came in and said she would take care of my mother as if she were her own. We gave Mother one last kiss and left her, one of the hardest things I have ever done. I know this sounds odd, but I felt like an orphan. I was parentless and I felt so alone. We made the calls, started the information chain for mother's many relatives, and drove home. We had already made arrangements for her cremation and I stayed for a few days to help my sister organize things. There was no funeral. We couldn't face it and Mother didn't want one. I am not sure any of us could have lived through it. This was the fifth family member I had lost in five years. It sent me into a tailspin of emotions again. I felt a void I wasn't sure could be filled. My dear mother, whom I loved so much, was gone. Who would I turn to when I needed advice? I felt like I was truly alone.

My niece gave birth to my great nephew, Matthew, less than a month after my mother died. Although Mom did not get to see him, that boy brought a ray of sunshine into our family, a much-needed moment of joy. He gave my sister something to live for and the happiness only a grandchild can provide. We lost our dear mother, but we gained a ray of sunshine in our lives with Matthew.

Chapter 20

Grand Canyon Day 7: Mile 132 to 144

"The glories and the beauties of form, color, and sound unite in the
Grand Canyon - forms unrivaled even by the mountains, colors that
vie with sunsets, and sounds that span the diapason from tempest
to tinkling raindrop, from cataract to bubbling fountain."
— John Wesley Powell

I woke up the next morning a bit apprehensive about kayaking, but
I had resolved to be kinder to myself and was going to do just that. I
ate breakfast and looked at my kayak that I loved so much and felt
like I was betraying it. The Diesel clearly wanted to be out paddling
and I was for some unknown reason I was nervous to get in the
boat. Carli saw me apprehensive on a rock and came over and
talked to me for a long time. One of the cool things about kayaking
is how many friends you have from all walks of life and age levels.
Carli was all of 18, but I consider her a dear friend. She listened to
me and said the right things and after packing and preparing we
were on the water by 8:00 am. Once in the boat and paddling, I felt
the same exhilaration and happiness that one gets from kayaking. I
had decided that I might swim, and would have to be okay with
that.

Whitewater kayakers fall over a lot, easier than one might
expect. You find yourself tightly strapped into this piece of plastic,
tucking up, and unable to get air. It is always amazing to me to see

Go Pro's of me upside down. I would have sworn I was under a good sixty seconds and yet only ten seconds ticked by on the old Go Pro. So the trick when you fall over is to roll back up. This is easier said than done. The whole rolling concept is based on Newton's Laws of Motion. This sounds easy enough with just three major steps, and quite a few smaller ones. Of course, the roll rarely works if one is panicked and rushing, a thing one tends to do when you can't breathe. The funny thing is I have an excellent roll, but it just seemed to take a vacation in the Canyon. No matter how hard I tried, I just could not get the boat to right itself.

The lesson here is this, you have to remain calm and trust yourself when you find yourself in adverse situations. Hanging on and counting to three is the best way to roll up when you are nervous, kind of like in life. Take a deep breath and wait a second before you attempt something you know you need your wits about you to do. Carli promised to hang out with me if I got behind in the group, and I found that I was enjoying kayaking again. I had a perfect day on the river. I came to terms with the fact I might swim, but maybe I would have a more successful day. Sometimes you have to listen to your friends and believe in yourself.

Chapter 21

Recovery

I went home to Georgia feeling lost and adrift again. This was four years after my husband had died. I had come a long way from the insecure, frightened, lonely woman I was. I had fought depression from the deaths and fear of losing more family members through being outdoors, mountain biking, hiking, kayaking and travelling and the great friendships I had made. Mom's death hit me in a way I had not expected. I didn't expect my sisters or husband, or Dennis to die. I had expected my mother would die someday, but the shock and loss still hit me hard. You go through a series of emotions that you wouldn't expect. Sadness obviously, but I felt guilt that I wanted it to be over to end her suffering as well as my own. I felt loneliness, even though I still had family members who loved me and a huge friend network. Finally the nightmares had returned. Jim nightmares again, Mom nightmares, nightmares that I was inadequate, unable to do things I loved doing, hearing that raspy labored breathing that awakened me from a dead sleep. The nightmares are always the hardest part of the grief process for me. Alone in the dark, nothing to take your mind off things, just the nightmares, always the nightmares.

I leapt back into kayaking with a vengeance to keep my mind occupied. I paddled 122 days in 2010. With paddling and with the friends I had in the paddling community, I found some much needed peace. I had to concentrate to paddle and could not think of other troubling things, and I found that after a day of kayaking, I could sleep from the exhaustion that only sports and exercise can bring. My kayaking skills were improving and as a result my confidence and self-esteem continued to improve. My friends and support network were still there and surrounded me with their friendship and helped to quell the intense pain of grief. One benefit of whitewater kayaking is that it is such an empowering sport. You support each other rather than compete as in many sports, so everyone cheers for you and your accomplishments. One of the best things a person can do for confidence is to pick a sport they love, and do it often. This also had a positive effect on my mental health and well-being as I experience success like I had never known before in my new chosen sport. The nightmares became less and less as the year went on, and I found I could finally do a crossword or remember my mother and smile instead of being only sad. Loved ones want you to remember them with laughter and fond memories, not tears.

The people that kayak are a diverse bunch, but the one thing they have in common is a crazy, unique sense of humor and love of life, which is infectious. Maybe it is the adrenaline nature of the sport that brings out that type of person, but paddling on the river, laughing with your friends, and enjoying all nature has to offer is the best healing you can partake in, a healing to your soul.

One mental burden I have not been able to overcome through all of this is overeating. I love food, everything about it. My weight went up 50 pounds from the time my mother starting getting sick until she finally died. I always have found comfort in food. Jim controlling my every diet did not help matters. I almost think food is a rebellion for me in some way, I could eat what I wanted and he couldn't say anything now. I still spend a great deal of time on eating and worrying about my weight. It is one demon I still have not been able to conquer. It is still an obstacle that I need to overcome to this day.

I had slowly been selling off things around the house, things I didn't need. I had an overwhelming need to rid myself of excess stuff. I felt the need to downsize. A single person does not need a house that is almost 3000 square feet on an acre to take care of. I had it on the market for years and it never sold. The housing market had dropped and a house with five cats in is doesn't show well. I often stayed at Freeman's Hotel near Bryson City, NC, when kayaking in the winter and the owner offered me a house I could rent in the non-winter months. My cats would be welcome. I remember the hesitation in his voice when he first told me about the house. We walked back behind his hotel property and I fell in love with that house, which affectionately became known as "the shack". A run down, dilapidated 100-year-old farmhouse stood in front of us. It had a small screened in foyer, huge covered porch on the back, one bedroom, two living rooms, full kitchen, and bath and a two-bedroom loft. Everything in the house was slightly on a slant and had that Grandma's basement kind of smell. The roof leaks in places (thankfully not over the couch or bed) and the floor was worn through in place. It was perfect for a summer kayaking haven. I couldn't wait to move in and the best part was now I would have a home in NC, except for the winters when he had to turn the water off to the exposed pipes wouldn't freeze over.

I went back to my Georgia house and started cleaning like crazy and selling stuff off. I figured with the cats out of there and the house more staged, it might sell. I hired a professional cleaning service to clean the house after I got out for the summer. The last day of school, I drove home, finished packing the truck, stuffed five screaming, unhappy cats into carriers and started off for NC. Cats don't travel well and the normally 2.5 hour pleasant drive turned into a nightmare of screaming, pissed off cats. It was worth it though to be in that NC house for the summer. Although the cats wanted to stay pissed at me, they just couldn't. A chipmunk family outside the kitchen window, birds galore, and new smells were like a vacation for them as well. They love that house and although they protest being shoved into the boxes each summer, they love the house as much as I do once they get there. That summer was perfect. I was right at the river so I could kayak, hike, explore, and hang out with friends every day. My life turned into a perfect pattern, paddle, hike, dinner with friends, on every weekend night at the pub by the river we would have beer, listen to live music, visit with friends, and have pizza. Life could not have been better.

A few weeks into summer I got a call from my realtor. A family was interested in the house. They couldn't get a mortgage yet but would do a lease- purchase plan for two years. They would move in in September. Now I needed a place to live and had to get ready to pack up. I drove home and looked around for a rental place to stay without any luck. Then I looked on Craig's list and found the perfect house, a slightly newer version of the house I had rented in in NC. It was a 100 year old farmhouse on about two acres in the middle of huge, expensive homes on ten acre lots. The farm had been subdivided, and this was the last structure in a great neighborhood much closer to my job. I was sold.

My husband loved our cats and when one died, it devastated him. He put their ashes in urns on a shelf in the den. He had asked to have his cremains placed on the shelf as well. I was feeling the need to take the next step in my recovery/healing process. I was not going to pack up the remains of my husband and cats in a cardboard box and move them in a box labeled husband and cats. I felt compelled to be rid of this chapter in my life and it was imperative that I do this to start my life refreshed. So I thought of a perfect place to spread all of their ashes. Jim loved Fort Mountain State Park. There was a bench with a beautiful view and it was a special place for us. So I put Jim's remains in a cardboard box. For those of you who have never dealt with human cremains, it is more than you would think, a huge plastic bag full. Then I opened up the cat urns and placed ten little Ziploc bags of cat ashes in the same box and headed out. This was a Monday so I figured who would be out at the park? As soon as I started on the mile or so hike, I realized I had not thought this through. I was carrying a large cardboard box in the woods, which was suspicious enough. What was worse is they were filled with little Ziploc bags of ashes with cats' names on them plus Jim's. I was sure I would be committed to a mental facility if a ranger stopped me and realized what I was carrying. I should have put them in a backpack. So I crept up the trail praying I wouldn't see anyone else. When I was almost to the spot to disperse the ashes, I heard voices, lots of voices, and most of them children. This is a nightmare situation. I snuck off the trail into the bushes, hid, and texted my sister, Leslie. Only she would find this as funny as I did. We have so many "ashes stories" and while morbid, all funny. Despite the precarious position I was in, I started to giggle uncontrollably, hidden behind a bush texting my sister, Leslie, who I am sure was doing the same thing down in Florida.

Years before, my sister and brother went to pick up my father's ashes. I didn't go because my husband didn't want me to and I didn't want to start a fight. My siblings got there and had ordered an urn. They walked out with this cardboard box and an urn. This was our first experience with just how many ashes there are from a cremation. So John and Leslie were in a dilemma. They did not want to upset Mom with the sight of all those ashes in a cardboard box, so they decided to spread some at all the firehouses where he had worked at in St. Petersburg. On the way to the first station the box tipped and some of the ashes hit the minivan floor. We never did tell mom what that stain was in the back. Leslie and John went to all the firehouses and sprinkled some of Dad in the places he liked best. The rest were spread at Ft. Desoto Park, my dad's favorite place.

When my first sister died in Texas her ashes were shipped to my sister's house via USPS. My sister said the look on the postman's face was priceless handing over that box containing the urn with the ashes, human remains was labeled on the outside. We had not had time to spread Diane's ashes when Karen passed, and once again my sister got a box of human remains mailed to her. My sisters were larger so my sister, Leslie, found places for my sister's ashes so my mom would not be faced with such a large quantity of ashes. When the time came we went to spread the girls' ashes at the same place in Ft. Desoto that my dad's were spread. We said our final goodbyes and put some ashes in the water and some by the same bench where we had spread our dad's. As kids we used to catch bait fish there with cast nests and spent untold numbers of hours fishing off that remote stretch overlooking the Sunshine Skyway Bridge. No one swims here and it is always deserted. It was such a beautiful and special place for us.

When we went to spread my mother's ashes there years later, we were expecting to be alone. But instead when John, Leslie, and I got there, there was a huge amount of people Kite Surfing. This involves huge kites and a surfboard you use to sail up into the air. There must have been 100 people leaping all over. I could almost hear mother giggling over the shock on our faces. What were we going to do? We had driven a long way to drop the ashes. There were people sitting on the bench where Mother wanted her ashes placed with Dad and the girls. My sister, Leslie, took charge. She grabbed a handful of Mom's ashes and nonchalantly walked over to the bench and as stealthily as she could dropped them at the bench by the feet of kite surfers taking a break. Of course, they noticed and John and I were snickering over by the car. We walked to the end of the land in the mangrove trees to spread the rest. We held hands and John and Leslie spread the ashes in the water. Mother was terrified of water, we could barely get her on a bridge. I was afraid she would come back and haunt me if I put her in the water. So I said my goodbyes and put her ashes in the thick of the mangrove trees with a perfect view of the golden, yellow arches of the Sunshine Skyway Bridge. Mom, Dad, Diane, and Karen's remains were resting in our special place.

Now as I'm hiding in the woods texting my sister, she too is laughing in Jacksonville. I am pretty sure if someone comes up on me now I will be arrested or at the very least committed. I am laughing so hard now I am crying. After what seemed like an eternity, the people finally left and I headed over to the bench. Now the moment was here and I wasn't sure how to say goodbye or if Jim would approve of this spot. But I finally made up my mind, opened the bag containing his ashes, stopped to admire the beautiful view and spread Jim's ashes over the hill. To my horror I now realized the entire hillside that sloped below me was covered in a fine white coating of ashes. It looked like it had snowed. Then to make matters worse, I looked down and saw a hospital identification bracelet way down in the middle of it all. I had to get it in case it had his name on it. Now I had to crawl down the steep side of the hill covered in ash to retrieve the bracelet that did indeed have his name, ID, and Social Security number on it. I still had the Ziploc bags of cats to spread. By the time I was done, it looked like it had snowed gray all over the mountain as far as you could see. I said my final good byes to Jim and my beloved cats. In spite of the mixed up, nutty time it took me to get here, I could not believe how beautiful it was. It almost took my breath away.

As I headed back to the car I was wondering how many perplexed people would stop at that bench over the next few days and wonder what all that grey stuff was all over the mountain since rain wasn't predicted for quite some time. Naturally Leslie thought this was the funniest thing she had heard in quite some time and I'm sure this provided her with giggles for quite a few days. One thing I have learned through all the grief and tragedy is to never pass up the opportunity to laugh. My sister and I sure had a hardy laugh over that day.

Summer ended and I felt better than I had in a long time. I was beginning to realize my heart and soul were in the Bryson City area of North Carolina and I hoped to be able to move there permanently someday. I moved all my stuff out of the house and to my new house. I felt an immense burden lift off my shoulders to be away from that house and huge mortgage. Yes, I still technically owned it, but was hopeful they could get a mortgage and buy it in two years. I had left a huge showplace house with granite countertops, all the extras, hardwood floors, and moved into a tiny fairly run-down old farmhouse and just felt like the weight of the world was off my shoulders. This was truly the first place I could call my own totally. I got rid of the plates, silverware, glasses, everything that was "us" and replaced them with things that were "me". I now was enjoying the thought of picking out my own things, from towels to shower curtains to new pictures on the wall. The old house had been so much "Jim" and I still felt him everywhere in that house. Every corner, decoration, tree, reminded me of him and I was oppressed by it. I felt a cleansing of the soul moving out of that house. This new house is also where I learned that a nice, fancy house isn't what makes you happy. A house isn't always a home. This little house I was renting was a home, my home. I picked it out, furnished it, decorated it, and made it mine, the first home I had since childhood I felt was truly mine. And to top it off, there was a professional pet sitter, Marla, who lives across the street and loves my cats as much as I do. Sometimes you just have to let go. The best thing you can do for yourself is start over. Get rid of things that oppress you, wipe the slate clean, and start over in new surroundings that you can call your own. I am still going through things that were "ours" and replacing them with things that are mine only.

Chapter 22

Day 8: Mile 144 to 165

"Life is like the river, sometimes it sweeps you gently along and sometimes the rapids come out of nowhere."
— Emma Smith

I would not have thought it possible to be as tired as I was. By day eight we had all reached a new level of dirtiness. I embraced the sand and rarely even made attempts to rid my feet of the microfine sand. I found I was actually enjoying it and felt that I was becoming one with the canyon both spiritually and physically. The constant heat, 20 + mile water days, hiking, and paddling were just tiring. I probably slept better than I have in my entire life on those cots right by the water, but going to sleep by eight and up at five every morning left me beyond tired, but a good kind of tired. I was in the raft when we got to Havasaui Canyon. I could see the azure blue water mixing with the muddy brown of the Colorado. We parked the rafts, ate our lunch huddled into whatever shade we could find, and began a hike. I thought the hikes here were brutal and to be honest avoided most of them, but the first leg of this one was a must. You could not stay on the rafts in the sun, it was simply too hot. With a little help from Wendy and Kari I picked my way up the rocks trying to avoid staying near the edge of the drop offs. It was actually an easy hike and then I saw the creek. For those of you who have never seen it, I just can't begin to describe it. The color has no name to adequately describe it. It doesn't look real. I decided to read my book at the first beach area while the others hiked. The cool packed sand was very comfortable. I lay down against my backpack by the clear water and before I knew it was sound asleep. I know people say that you need expensive mattresses and soft pillows to sleep, but I can tell you that two hour nap I had on the cool sand on the bank of the creek with my head on a lumpy backpack was one of the best, most peaceful, and restful sleeps I have ever had.

Since I had not kayaked in the morning, I decided to put in after the hike and paddle a bit. I made it through the first two rapids and then swam. My only regret in the canyon is that whenever I swam I got back into the raft and didn't try to paddle any more. One should not see a set back as a failure. Easier said than done, I know, but every swim I perceived as a failure and I just gave up on paddling, probably the thing I love most in the world. I often take private kayak instruction lessons with Juliet. We have a unique relationship on the water. She always believes in me and pushes me whether I want to or not, and I can be difficult. Whenever I swim when she's around, she makes me get out in the current and roll, kicking and crying sometimes, but I do it and always feel better about it. I should have followed her example in the canyon and motivated myself to go out there and try again instead of shutting down on rolling all together. Always surround yourself with people who know you can achieve whatever you wish to accomplish and then make you do it. Sometimes a gentle push is all you need to achieve your greatness. In retrospect I should have stayed in the kayak instead of quitting. Self-motivation is still difficult for me, but I am persistent and will keep going after I've had some time to reflect on my mistakes and perceived failures. I was worried that everyone was put out by my swimming and that made me get in the raft instead of trying again. Since my day six meditation day, I was, however, okay with the raft trip. I wasn't beating myself up for swimming and just enjoyed the raft trip. I found that once again, Andrea's favorite statement, "You have to find your own happiness," was true. I found myself smiling and enjoying the company of Art who normally was on the raft with me, exchanging stories and enjoying the scenery.

We pulled into a place called Tuck Up Canyon to camp. Most of our campsites had been fairly small but this one had a secluded beach a bit away and I figured a perfect place to take a real bath. It also had a slot canyon that you could explore. I had never skinny dipped before, but the thought of getting everything off and really scrubbing up was very appealing. The water was full of silt and brown but so was I and most of what I owned, so I set off with Carli and Nancy, towel and soap in hand. It took me a while to get the guts up to strip down and jump in, but I did. The feeling of being naked floating around in that water was actually quite enjoyable, my first skinny dip. I kept expecting a raft full of people to come around the bend, but it never did. Totally soaped up and rinsed. I felt somewhat cleaner than I had when I started. One more thing off my bucket list, skinny dipping.

Chapter 23

Find Your Own Happiness

Through all this trauma, tragedy, and grief the one thing I strongly think is the key to recovery and happiness in life is that you have to decide to be happy and take steps to do so, especially when life appears to have other things in mind for you. I hate the phrase, "God only gives you what you are able to handle." Really? That always feels to me there is some divine power trying to stick it to me. Why do I deserve more badness in the world than others? Just because I am stronger? If that were the case, I would strongly encourage everyone to be a wimp and be weak so you don't get handed these burdens, which frankly I don't think anyone can take without some form of depression and overwhelming sadness and grief. Instead, I think these events are just random events that we have to face as we live on this planet. Everyone is born and eventually has to die. If you have family, friends, or loved ones, you will be faced with someone's death eventually. I have an extremely large family and friend network so by default more people I love will die. In my opinion it is worth it. I would rather be surrounded by love of family and friendship and take the chance of losing them than never having had the experience.

I make the choice to be happy. Most of the things you deal with in life come down to the choices we make and the choices we make dealing with adversity. I deal with the losses I have been dealt in the usual fashion: Denial, Anger, Bargaining, Depression, and Acceptance. But I tend to go through them quickly and still try to enjoy life while dealing with them until I get to the acceptance part. I still think it's normal to fall back into depression and insecurities at times and I still fluctuate between confidence, lack of confidence, happiness, and sadness. It is hard not to go into denial when your sister calls you just four months later and tells you another sister is dead. But after the initial shock and anger at losing another person, I moved to depression and acceptance at the same time. Once again, it is a choice. People are not always ready to move on as quickly. I have dealt with so many deaths I feel like the best strategy is to grieve quickly, like pulling of a Band-Aid. That doesn't mean you stay in denial, but you just decide to live your life while remembering your loved ones and find happiness wherever you can while honoring their memory.

I make a choice to remember my loved ones with laughter and not sadness. I do sometimes shed a tear now and then when the pain of not having them in my life feels raw or holidays seem unbearable. But then I remember the happiness they brought to my life, and happiness is more necessary than sadness. It's as important as breathing. I would like to think my relatives that are gone would want me to be happy and remember them with goofiness and silliness like we did when they were alive. They gave me a lifetime of happy memories. I hate the thought of only remembering them with sadness and unhappiness. Their lives meant more to me than that.

I also made a choice to heal as quickly as possible and to avail myself of whatever would help me do so. I went to therapy for grief, and sometimes anxiety, and self-confidence issues more than once over the years. I have never heard of therapy hurting anyone. It is amazing to me what a sense of relief it is to share your burdens with someone else who isn't family and won't judge you. Why wouldn't you get all the help you can get to deal with grief and sadness? If you get a broken arm, you go to an orthopedist to get it fixed. So if your heart is broken, why don't you go to a counselor who specializes in that and can get you on the road to recovery? I have always felt great relief and comfort in counseling. Doing everything you can to make yourself happy is just smart, not a sign of weakness.

Something else that helps me be happy is to remember my lost loved ones frequently. I make a point to remember them with fondness and hardly a day goes by that I don't think of one of them, my dad's love of outdoors, my mom's love of puzzles and a good beer, my sister Dianne in that silly blue bunny suit and her love of reading, my sister Karen liking all things cows. I still can't pass a *Chik-Fil-A* cow's billboard without remembering Karen with a smile on my face. I think of them all and am so glad they enriched my life and try to repay that with happy memories and smiles. I had such joy with them while they were living, so I choose to still be with them in my thoughts and continue to live with them. When you cry or grieve for someone that has passed, you aren't really grieving for them. Your loved one is no longer in pain, suffering, or unhappy regardless of your beliefs in the afterlife, they are certainly at peace. You cry for yourself, the terrible ache and loneliness created in your soul and heart by their absence, you cry for the "missing" of all things that made them good. In reality those things are still there inside you. They might not be where you can physically "see" them, but believing is in the feeling, not the seeing. My father is with me every day as surely as if he was sitting right next to me. His love, experiences, philosophies, everything that made my father wonderful, lives inside me. The greatest compliment someone can give me is to say "You are just like your mom," or "You are the spitting image of your father." Every time I get in a kayak or fly fish, my father is right there with me. My sisters and all my departed family members shaped my life with their love and will always live inside me and made me who I am today.

My niece gave birth to a baby girl in 2013, Meiomi, who reminded my family and me to love life and cherish every moment we have together. Meiomi lived just seven short days and I never got to hold her or meet her, but she touched my family and me just the same. The love my niece, Kelly, and her husband, felt towards that baby filled a lifetime in just seven short days. Kelly chose to cherish her life and her memory with happiness and to be thankful for the short time they had together. It was the most difficult thing someone has to face, especially someone so young, but she handled it with grace, compassion, and love, a lesson for all of us. So thank you, Mei, for reminding us in your short life to love and cherish our family and enjoy the precious time we have.

On a lighter note, one of the most important things to being happy is having the ability to laugh at yourself. I have been known to do some pretty silly things and maybe just maybe overreact slightly to the difficulty or hazards of certain whitewater rapids. This sometimes makes me the butt of jokes and comments. You just have to be able to laugh at yourself in these times. We all do things we might feel are not overly bright or smart, but sure felt right at the time. When people laugh with you or at you in a friendly teasing way, it sure helps to laugh back. Laughing also can brighten your mood and certainly the mood of those around you. I laugh a bunch, sometimes at the silliest things, and it just makes you feel joyful.

Which goes along with don't take life so seriously. Kid around, laugh a bit and if you do something stupid and someone laughs, laugh too! Join in on the fun instead of just being a sourpuss. Wear stupid costumes on Halloween, wear purple toe nail polish, or sign up for a mud run or other running event even if you have to walk the whole thing. You will find you will keep more friends and enjoy them more if you have a light, jovial mood and laugh frequently. There are so many things you can do to make yourselves happy, but you have to get off the couch, get out, surround yourself with friends, and find your happy activity.

Chapter 24

Day 9: Miles 165 to 176

"The earth has music for those who listen."
— George Santayana

The slot canyon in the campground had a great hike in it. We set off early for the rock scramble into the canyon. It is sobering to see those boulders the size of houses tumbled all over the place like tiny pebbles and realize those things came down in a torrent of water washing into the canyon. The slot canyons are the sites of incredible flooding and to witness such an event must be indescribable. Those boulders presented something of a challenge for me. I have this thing about walking on rocks and climbing; it scares me, but by this day, I was fine. My confidence was growing and I did the complete hike, quite a ways back to a small pool of water where the canyon went straight up from this point. Things in the canyon are on a grand scale and this place was no exception. Huge walls jutted up around us and loose boulders from unforeseen flash floods dotted the landscape. The sun hadn't hit the canyon yet, so it was still cool and we enjoyed the first hike of the day.

Lava Falls is the largest rapid on the Grand Canyon and the guide and other people on our trip wanted to hit it at the highest water level which would be early in the morning. So it was decided that we would do a short paddle day and camp early so we could hit Lava at maximum flow. This would be a loafing kind of day. We premade our lunch sandwiches in anticipation of a lunch hike.

After a very short paddle, we arrived at National Canyon. This would be a short hike into another slot canyon, albeit larger, where we could sit in the shade, swim in a pool, and read for a while. I took a dip in the clear water and rinsed my hair in the small cascading waterfall that made up the pool.

Wet, so now I had natural air conditioning, I enjoyed a lazy afternoon reading, napping, and visiting with my friends in the shade. This canyon had also been the site of a flash flood a few years back. One day the canyon was clear, the next it was littered with house -size boulders. Imagine the force of that water as it carried the debris roaring down the canyon. Thankfully no one was there at the time and imagine the surprise of the rafting company who came upon it one morning and saw such a dramatically different landscape.

It was a fun day paddling and when we arrived at camp, I was looking forward to a relaxing evening. I was having the time of my life, but was so exhausted from the heat, paddling, and hiking. It is amazing to me how 20 people are all in bed and pretty much asleep by 8:30 as soon as the sun sets. On my beach front cot, I was getting very used to sleeping to the sound of the rushing Colorado, covered in a blanket of stars, and watching the many bats eat their nighttime meals swooping over my head, some of them quite close. People are meant to be outdoors. Closed up in concrete and air conditioning is an unnatural place to be. I slept so well out there and without a care in the world. I realized I had stopped biting my nails and felt healthier than I had in some time. Nature has a healing power all of its own and immersing myself in it for 12 days was certainly having a positive effect on me.

Chapter 25

The Healing Power of the Outdoors

So what can people do to make themselves happier in life? There is nothing more cathartic than to be in the outdoors. My classroom at work doesn't even have a window. Sometimes if I am very stressed, which often happens teaching middle school, I just step outside and stand under a tree on break, close my eyes, and listen to the birds in the trees, the rustle of the leaves in the wind, the smell of flowers, or the crisp air. I can feel the tension melt away. I have been known to take unruly, squirrely classes for a walk around the building and back. This does wonders for middle school heebie jeebies. This is why I feel it is so awful that Physical Education Classes are being cut back in the schools. Kids spend precious little time outside anymore. They need to get out of the building at least once a day and get some fresh air.

A daily walk can make you feel refreshed and eager to face the day. I feel myself relax, tension leaving my body, my soul at peace. When you take a walk enjoy all of your senses. Sometimes just stop and listen to the sounds. You will be amazed how many beautiful and soothing sounds you will hear from birds, insects, wind in the leaves. Every living thing has a unique sound that has a song of its own. Close your eyes and listen.

While your eyes are closed, open your mouth and taste the air. Crisp mountain air, salty beach air, water droplets from humidity, the smells from the flowers, honeysuckle, all give off a taste in the air.

Touch, feel the texture of the leaves, the roughness and smoothness of the bark, the feel of sand/dirt/mud between your toes, the feel of the grasses and other plants. Feel the breeze blow your hair and caress your face.

Smell the flowers, plants, air. Enjoy the different fragrances and smells that you can only have outside. We often live in air conditioned houses, rarely opening windows, isolated from the fresh air which has a smell that connects us to nature and heals and relaxes us. I live in a house without central air conditioners just north of Hotlanta. Know what? I sleep just fine with fans and open windows, and I save a ton on electricity while enjoying nature.

The last sense is sight, the obvious one, but instead of just looking at the colors and sights, really see them, the dew on a spider web, the different hues of green and other colors, the way clouds make shapes and so do trees, leaves. Watch the way tree trunks bend to get to the light, the way the sunlight streaks through the branches from the forest canopy to the floor. Enjoy the beauty of the outdoors.

Don't be in such a hurry to get where you are going that you don't enjoy your present location. One evening in North Carolina I got home late, very tired, and it was pitch black out without any light pollution. I glanced up and saw a blanket of stars covering the entire sky. I was tired and it had been a long day, but I popped the tail gate down on my truck and lay there looking up at the unbelievable beauty above me. The trees were full of fireflies and looked like someone had decorated the tall trees with strings of silver and white sparkling Christmas lights. It was one of the most beautiful sights I had ever seen. I must have spent 30 minutes or so out there lying in the bed of my pickup truck looking up at the heavens. It was incredibly peaceful. Never be in too much of a hurry to stop and look at the stars, smell the roses, enjoy the scenery. When driving somewhere on vacation, don't get so focused on getting to a place that you bypass the scenic overlooks, cool mom and pop establishments, eating outside on picnic tables, or just side trips enjoying the great outdoors.

Have you ever been alone somewhere outdoors? Truly alone? It is almost magical. I love to go on short hikes into the woods alone, find a rock, sit there, close my eyes, and just take it all in. For someone who is always busy like I am, both work wise and body motion wise, which is the most calming thing imaginable. I really try to look at the rocks, trees, leaves, flowers, air, sky, clouds, water, so many things that you just don't notice in the company of others. You tend to focus on them and have conversations and then you miss out on the sounds of nature. Sometimes you need to converse with nature as much with people.

Once I found myself alone on Jaco Beach in Costa Rica before 7:00am. I'm an early riser and wanted to watch the first rays of sun hit the beach. We were on the Pacific side, so the sun rose behind me as I stared at the water. I was standing ankle deep feeling the water lap against me and my toes and feet sink into the sand as I wiggled my toes. The different shades of colors were magnificent as they shown on the water and sand of the beach. The cry of gulls and the lapping of the surf were just indescribable. I stood there for quite some time, people started coming and I lost the total solitude. But for that perfect moment in time, I was the only one on the beach, the planet, anywhere. You just feel all the tension melting away and a peace come over you when you take the time to commune with nature like that. I find myself an early riser on vacations so I don't miss moments like this.

Years later on another Costa Rica trip, I was also up with the sunrise walking on that same beach, but there were many people on this day and for some reason they were looking down. I noticed police officers standing there picking something up. To my delight, I realized the beach was crawling with newly hatched sea turtles. They were sheparding the last of them to the safety of the ocean. I found myself in the midst of Costa Ricans, Germans, and people from all walks of life helping the turtles reach safety. I asked the police officer in my growing Spanish if I could help. He eagerly gave me latex gloves and I helped the last ones into the sea. What an amazing experience to witness such a miracle, to hold a turtle a few hours old as he bravely tried to get to the ocean. I wished them luck as I put them in the surf and watched them scamper off into the crashing waves. The odds are against them, but thanks to us every one of the hatchlings made it to the ocean safely.

You can't think of outdoors without thinking about sports. I know what some of you are thinking, you are as far from an athlete as can be. Know what? So am I, but it doesn't matter. There are many sports to choose from that will meet the needs of any person. You don't have to be good or Olympic quality, you just have to get out there and do it. While I started out mountain biking and found that one wasn't really for me, I have also enjoyed hiking, walking, fly fishing, and kayaking. There is certainly something for everyone, take the time to try them all. When my sister started exercising, she found unexpectedly at the age of 52 that she likes running/walking 5k's. She liked the challenge of improving her time and the camaraderie of the other runners. She has since progressed up to half marathons. While I dislike running and competing in running races, it fits her well. I do walk/run 5K's with her when I go to visit. And I finished my first half marathon, the Donna 13.1 in Jacksonville, and felt a tremendous sense of accomplishment. Try different outdoor activities, sporting clubs, and events till you find the one that fits. When you exercise, you release endorphins that improve your mood and make you feel good. Nothing will brighten your mood and lift your sprits like a walk. You will find the more activities that you do outside, the better you will feel. I feel that participating in these outside activities has had a huge impact on my mental state and adds to my happiness and quality of life.

My father's birthday is July 19th and a few years ago I was missing him terribly. One of my fondest memories with my father was fishing. We spent many hours fishing in the gulf, bays, and oceans of Florida. In addition to kayaking, Endless River Adventures offers fly fishing instruction, so I decided to ask Ken to teach me to fly fish. Once again I found a peaceful, albeit complicated, outside sport that I can do alone or with others. I find it very challenging to figure out the casting, types of flies, how to catch the different types of fish, and the challenge of setting the hook and landing a fish. It is difficult to learn and very rewarding when you catch a fish. To watch someone good fly fish is like an art form. And while I look nothing like Ken when he casts, it doesn't really matter. I'm outside in the water enjoying nature and learning new things every time I go out. I was happy to add one more outdoor activity to my list of things I like to do. I feel like I honor the memory of my father every time I cast that rod and enjoy fishing. This year when I was out fishing, I finally caught my first brown trout, an 18 incher! Ken, Bob, and I were in the raft on the Nantahala River when the brown hit the nymph. The boys know immediately it was a Brown Trout and started giving me directions while Ken rowed the raft to an eddy. Bob jumped out with a net and the Brown was still fighting. I did everything they told me and saw it break the surface and in the net. I couldn't believe I had landed an 18 inch brown trout and what a fight he put up. We do catch and release, so after pictures we made sure the trout was returned to live another day.

An unexpected side effect of my new love of outdoors is that I find I can't stand air conditioning anymore. I want to feel the fresh breeze and hear the sounds of the nocturnal animals singing the night away. My summer house in North Carolina is more of a shack, with holes in the floor and leaky ceilings in unimportant locations, but it allows me to live in one of the most beautiful places on earth during the summer months. I sleep so well there with the frogs, insects and even the squirrels playing a night game of "tackle" or "keep away" on my metal roof. I have a window unit in my home in Georgia, but rarely turn it on. I would rather be hot then isolated from outdoors. Some nights I get rewarded with the hoot of an owl, along with the normal nighttime song. My soul is at peace hearing those sounds as I drift off to sleep in a nightmare free slumber finally.

As our lives have become more complex, busier, and more isolated from the outdoors, it seems we have lost some vital connections with nature. Maybe regaining some of those severed ties with the outdoors will return us to the pleasures of being outside and enjoying nature and reduce the stress and anxiety so many of us are feeling.

Chapter 26

Day 10: Mile 176 to 213

The river delights to lift us free, if only we dare to let go.
Our true work is this voyage, this adventure.
— Richard Bach, *Illusions: The Adventures of a Reluctant Messiah*

Up and early we hit the water by 8:00. I had pretty much decided that I was not going to kayak Lava Falls Rapid. It had mattered so much to me back home and in the planning that I was sure that not running it would upset me greatly. However, that changed once I first heard it. The light hadn't hit the canyon yet and I was enjoying the shadows playing on the canyon walls in the silence of the morning as we were all still waking up. The oranges, purples, magenta, and yellows were all moving around the canyon as the sun came up. It was serenely peaceful until we rounded a corner. At first I thought something was wrong, a plane crash, flash flood, something to make that roar. Then I realized we must be approaching Lava Falls.

We got out of our kayaks to scout it and watch 4 people run it from the top. I will never forget the moment of seeing that rapid, the Holy Grail of big water kayaking, the rapid that we have heard about since we started kayaking. It was massive. Exploding waves was an understatement. We watched Dave, Craig, Zoe, and Meghan enter the rapid. They all appeared to be right on target, then Zoe just disappeared. One minute her boat was there and the next sucked under. I was trying to find her red boat when I saw Meghan's Green boat shoot out of the air like it was nothing, no small feat for a 12 foot boat. Then as I watched Zoe reappear and roll up, Meghan again shot out of the water. After seeing everyone safe at the bottom of the rapid, I hightailed it to the raft, strapped my kayak on and got ready for a fun ride in the "bathtub" section of the raft. Chris, Rob, Wendy, and I sat in the front and held on. You can't see a thing from the top of the rapid, just a horizon line. As we dropped over the top I have never ever been so glad to not be in a kayak. The ride was incredible. Huge breaking, exploding waves engulfed us as we went down the rapid, laughing maniacally. It is very rare when you need to be wearing nose plugs on a raft, but we found ourselves totally submerged in the roar of the rapid.

I normally beat myself up for not running rapids and see it as an epic failure, but not this time. I was learning some things in the canyon that I hoped would stick. Yes, I was disappointed. Who wouldn't be when you so desperately wanted to do something, but I was content and happy with my choice. I got back in the water to paddle after Lava and had an enjoyable afternoon, focusing on my accomplishments instead of perceived failures.

The evening campsite was a place called Pumpkin Springs, an awesome camp site with tons of room right on the water and the springs, which I thought would be great for swimming had arsenic in it. The guides, Dom and Rachel, told us about a cliff jumping spot. I have never jumped off anything higher than a low diving board. As I've mentioned, I'm a bit of a chicken and afraid of heights. A month before, some friends and I had gone to Queen's Lake to watch the super moon from stand up paddle boards and some were jumping off the high dock into the water. Not me.

For some reason jumping off that 18 foot cliff looked appealing. So I soaped up my hair (figured the jump would wash the soap out), put on my PFD and up we went. I watched a few people jump off and once again, Matt had the best one liner of the day. "I guess this answers the question if all your friends jumped off the cliff, would you?"

Apparently the answer was yes. I got to the edge and to my great surprise actually leaped off with a smile on my face. It was incredible!!! Even more amazing is that I got back up the cliff side, which was virtually a difficult climb back up the cliff with no nerves or doubt. Even Zoe was amazed. Sometimes you just need to take a leap of faith and jump off that cliff. It was so much fun and I look forward to jumping off more cliffs in the future.

Chapter 27

Oh, The Friends You Meet

I know many people who have experienced death and not coped well. Why do some do well and others sink into depression? I am sure the answers are very complicated and there is certainly not one easy answer. But when I look back on all the trauma I have experienced over the last eight years, it is my friends that have made the biggest difference in my life. There always seems to be a friend nearby when I need them most to talk to, make me smile, laugh, or just hang out together. A true friend will let you call them at 1:00 in the morning crying and make you feel better. True friends are always there for each other. I make a conscious choice to seek friends out, socialize and get out of the house even when I don't feel like it, and to be a good friend myself.

I first realized this when my husband died and my team at work, Glenn, Debbie, Julie, and Sue were there for me every step of the way. They, along with the rest of the faculty, helped me cope with such a devastating loss. Since that first loss, my friends have always been there for me. Bright spots in dark times.

During my marriage I had no close friends; my husband was the only person I had any contact with. Now that I was on my own and making friends, I realized how much I had missed the close contact and camaraderie I had shared with my childhood friends. I was making up for lost time and quickly realizing the real key to happiness was to surround yourself with friends.

There are many kinds of friends that can enrich your life. Some are tried and true, best buddy type friends, the ones you call up when you need a shoulder to cry on, a sympathetic ear, the people you call first. These are few and far between. They always understand you and never judge you. You will find yourself laughing over the stupidest things and only you two understand. When you are at your darkest moments, they know exactly what to say to cheer you up. These people you call first when you need a sympathetic ear. Sometimes it seems they know you need them before you do and will call you to check on you. You feel your soul lighten and your spirits brighten when you are with them.

Then there are casual friends and work friends, the ones we hang out with in special situations that can make you smile. These friends are much more numerous and can make or break your workday. I always feel when I hear, "Good morning, how was your weekend?" from friends and colleagues, my day goes much better. They remember your birthday and bring in cake, celebrate your milestones and make every day good.

You also have the acquaintance people and Facebook friend people. You might only see these people occasionally or chat on Facebook once in a while, but you still have a sense of belonging and they add happiness to your life. They fill the little voids in your life with conversation, humor, and companionship.

You can never have too many friends and people that brighten your day. If you find you don't have enough people in your life that you can laugh with, you need to find an activity, sport, gym, or interest group that could increase the amount of people in your circle of friends. Nothing can lift depression and unhappiness like visiting and spending time with friends.

Taking a cruise would not be a vacation you would think would appeal to me, but my friends Kit, Gail, Collin, and her Mom Suzy and I went on a cruise to the Bahamas. I had such a good time. Sure the cruise activities were fun and the shore excursions a great experience from the sailboat/snorkeling cruise to the kayaking through the mangroves, but the real enjoyment was spending time with my friends. On the mangrove kayaking trip, an overly friendly raccoon decided it wanted my sandwich and just crawled up my leg. I must admit I didn't know those things had such sharp claws and I was bleeding. My friends (after enjoying a good laugh), found the first aid supplies and fixed me up. For the rest of the trip I endured, "Look out for the raccoons." We enjoyed copious amounts of chocolate in every form at the midnight chocolate buffet, lost money gambling, and watched all the cheesy dance and ventriloquist shows. Who can forget Collin's Hillary Clinton haircut, or Kit's legendary humor and that bucket of beer? I found out that Gail could sleep and read all day, probably much needed rest for a single mom of two boys. Basically we had the time of our lives, just unending laughter. It was the friendship that made that cruise so special.

Through kayaking I realize that age has no impact on who your friends are. I met Zoe through kayaking. She was 16 and a much better kayaker than I am. She had attended New River Academy and had kayaked in South America and Africa. Zoe took me under her wing and enjoyed teaching me to kayak, which was quite the undertaking. Saying I wasn't a natural at kayaking would be an understatement. Zoe was always patient and good at teaching and whenever I had an out-of-boat experience, otherwise known as an unplanned swim, she just smiled and helped me get back in. Zoe's bright and enthusiastic youthful exuberance was good for me. I saw things as she saw them, bright and fresh. Her mother once told me she was thankful Zoe ended up with a second mother. I must admit I was proud as could be to watch her walk in her high school graduation, get accepted into college, and start her academic life on campus. I would gladly call her my daughter. Watching her go through the typical passages of youth refreshed me and gave me an added zest toward life. From Olivia's first run of Nantahala Falls at the ripe old age of 10, to watching Carli (another adopted daughter) go from a scared unconfident paddler to a really good confident class 4 paddler who brightens every river with her smile, or Greta learning to do a loop, the young people I paddle with have certainly enriched my life. I paddle with people from nine to seventy nine and consider all of them my friends. I learn to appreciate life, see things through new eyes and a different perspective, and find new joys in life. Having friends regardless of age is important to be happy.

Then there is the "Juice Box Gang." I am not sure exactly how they acquired that name but feel it has something to do with the ever present juice boxes we get on the river with our lunches in Ecuador. The "Gang" consisted of men that would become my main paddling group and am honored that they call me friend. Tom, Carli's dad, is one of my strongest supporters and one of the few guys I can talk to about things bothering me. He listens and always has sage advice for me. I feel I have become a part of his family and you can never have enough family. David, another member, has three adorable children and the driest, sarcastic sense of humor I have ever seen. I can't get on the river without him making me smile. Connor is the reliable one, the one I can count on to help me with rapids, lend an ear or offer paddling suggestions. Describing Mark would require another book in itself. "Over the Top" is the best description for him. Cliff rounds out the bunch, the one who when in doubt he is the one to follow down a river. He is a conservative boater who knows all the easy lines and can make a difficult rapid an easy one. Alp was a late comer to the Gang, but his crazy paddling style, unending faith in my kayaking abilities, even when I didn't have them in myself, and his ability to paddle the most difficult situations then fall over in some flat water rapid makes him unique. This Gang and many others certainly enriched my life. A day paddling with "The Gang" is one I will walk away with smiling, an increased sense of accomplishment, and drive home light hearted and smiling. What more could you ask for from friends?

Juliet, in addition to being my kayaking instructor and friend, also holds the role of social coordinator for myself and many others. She introduced me to three women that were starting out kayaking and need a mentor, someone to help them learn and to be safe with while learning to paddle. She introduced me to Stephanie, Erica, and Nell, and the four of us really hit it off. I enjoyed spending time with those ladies and teaching them to kayak. Having them look up to me as the more experienced one was really good for my self-confidence. They trusted me to teach them to kayak and get them safely down the river. That meant a lot to me. The friendship I have with those ladies has led to so many happy times. I am so lucky to have such great friends. Stephanie and I really became close. Many days we have spent on the river fishing each other out from swims, offering encouragement, and the most important things, laughter and friendship. A true friend is one you can be absolutely silly with and be yourself.

It came time to run a river that was my first solid class 4 creek. When I decided to go, the person I wanted most to go with was Dennis Huntley and he brought Bob along for support. Dennis is near 70 and Bob is 16, an unlikely pair, but both are excellent paddlers and I had the time of my life that day with them. Don't discount making friends with someone just because they are in a different age bracket especially in sports. You might miss out on someone who will enrich your life in untold ways.

Different people teach you different things. I must admit the thought of ever getting married or involved with another man scares me. I was not sure I would ever be able to trust someone. Then I met Keith and Andrea. They are the happiest couple I have ever seen. The love they have for each other and life in general is infectious. I just can't help but smile and be happy when I am with them. They kayak with me and a day with them is a great, fun day regardless of where you are. I realized watching them that not all guys are bad. I often joke with Andrea that someday I hope to find my Keith.

Another person that taught me a great deal was Joel. Joel is the 17 year old son of a friend of mine in Ecuador, Angel. Joel got a visa and Juliet and Ken brought him over for nine weeks to the United States. I am not sure if anyone from the US can imagine what a wonderful shock and unique experience that is for someone from Ecuador to visit here. Ecuador certainly doesn't have the same standard of living that we enjoy in the US as the world sees it. He had to go through customs alone in Miami. Everyone speaks Spanish there so that wasn't too bad, but I can't imagine how much guts it took for him to board a US airline alone and come to Atlanta on his adventure. I knew he was coming and I had only met him briefly in Ecuador. I found him the next morning, barely twelve hours after arriving in the US, sitting in an office at ERA. I was with some friends and literally drug him out of the office, got him geared up and took him down the Nantahala River in a ducky. I was with Andrea, Keith, and Mazy, one of the most fun groups ever. Between my bad Spanish and his almost non-existent English, we had an awesome time. Then we kidnapped him to go tubing at Deep Creek in the Great Smokey Mountains National Park. I can only wonder what he thought of all these shenanigans on his first day in the United States. We took him to dinner for his first meal in the US, and saw the shock on his face at the prices and unending choices on the menu. We narrowed it down to carne, and he had a New York Strip. I hope I made his first US day memorable and happy. I took him out every weekend in a kayak and he got better faster than anyone I've ever seen. He was determined. He was appreciative of the time I spent with him and the help I gave him learning English. Teaching ESL was a big advantage here. He reciprocated with Spanish lessons. Often I would hear, "Mary, please repeat," as we paddled and I struggled valiantly to say the RR sound.

Joel appreciates everything and it was refreshing to see his view on all the new experiences he was having. I took him down the Ocoee River for the first time in a kayak, after only six weeks of paddling. Normally that takes a bit longer, but he had the time of his life and was all smiles. Andrea and Keith were there for support and then we camped out. The next day I took him to the Chattanooga Aquarium. Everyone should go to the aquarium once with someone who never has been to one. The look of wonder on his face cannot be described. He stood by the huge aquarium and just watched the sharks and fish for an hour, asking me many questions about them. Five hours later we left the aquarium, my Spanish and his English greatly improved. He just enjoys the things we frequently take for granted.

The things we think are necessities like *iPhones, iPads,* a computer and TV in every room are luxuries to Joel. We walked into my "shack" one night and it was so beautiful out. We just stopped to stare at the stars in wonder. We popped the tailgate down and sat there looking at the stars and fireflies for quite some time. I explained constellations, pointing out Betelgeuse the red star, and just looking. Never ever pass up the opportunity to look at a star filled sky. Joel had nine weeks with us before he returned to Ecuador. I felt like a rock star taking him down the rivers since he looked up to me as this awesome kayaker and instructor and he trusted me. His sense of wonder and excitement at even the smallest things really made me see the rivers and places through new eyes. Things don't make you happy, they can sometimes make your life so complicated and muddled that it can mask happiness. I saw in Joel the pure enjoyment one gets from discovering new things and spending time with new friends.

My many friends come from all walks of life and are as diverse as the flora in a rain forest. They are quirky, serious, conservative, liberal, religious, not so religious, funny, odd, and from every walk of life. Some are like me and some are entirely different from me. Why would you want to surround yourself with people just like you? It is the differences and unpredictableness of your friendships that bring you so much joy. Your only criteria for a friend should be that they treat you with respect and kindness, make you laugh, and they are always there for you.

In my darkest and most insecure moments, I know that I could always turn to a friend to listen to me. There are ups and downs when dealing with grief and recovery. It is not a linear process. Sometimes I feel on top of the world; then some memory or anniversary will occur and I find myself in a dark place, sad. I will call up a friend and talk and find most times the darkness lifts quickly. I choose to have as many friends as possible. I cannot imagine how sad my life would be without my friends.

Chapter 28

Day 11: Mile 213 to 246

"The purpose of life is to live it, to taste experience to the utmost,
to reach out eagerly and without fear for newer and richer
experience."
— Eleanor Roosevelt

I woke up this morning sad. This would be my last day paddling on
the canyon. I had been preparing for this trip for months and now
the last day was here. I hadn't swum in a while and was determined
that I would end this trip on a positive note. The last day was a
perfect day. We paddled in super fun wave trains and they weren't
as intimidating as they were at the start. I had learned to accept the
Colorado River and go with it, not try to change it or make sense of
it. It was what it was, a large turbulent river that although dammed
in many places was wild and free, almost a living entity, and it
wasn't interested in my expectations of how it should behave.

At mile 240 we came to Separation Canyon. Here on August 28,
1869, on the Powell expedition, three men decided they could take
no more and would hike out of the canyon. I can only imagine what
Powell and his men had come to deal with every day. The river was
not dammed then, but wild and free. The uncertainties, unknown
rapids, and constant danger led these three men to try to hike out.
Powell wrote that there were tears when the men left and they
watched them fade out of sight hoping they would join them again,
but they did not. They were never seen again. No one knows what

happened to those three men, but I thought of them there at that canyon. I could almost see them there making the tough decision to try to hike out of the canyon and try to make it home. What were they thinking as they watched Powell float away downstream and realized they were on their own in such a harsh and yet beautiful place? I hope their remains are somewhere in the confines of this canyon, resting in such a magical and beautiful place.

After Hoover Dam was constructed Lake Mead was formed and Lave Cliff Rapid, not to be confused with Lava Falls Rapid, was forever consumed by the rising waters of Lake Mead. We camped at Spencer Canyon. Lake Mead is now at the lowest level it has ever been. Lower rainfalls and less snow melt have made the river drop since its all-time high in the 80's. What was once a high water lake was now way below its banks. The campsite where we were to stay had once been at water level and now was quite a climb up from the rafts. We made a line of every person on the trip to pass our gear, bags, and kitchen up the hill for the night. When Dom was bringing out the crate of snacks, we noticed we had had a visitor on the raft, a beautiful black and white king snake. Wonder how long he'd been there. Did he perhaps chase the mouse we had been hearing onto the raft? He surely must have had a nice dinner because we never saw the mouse again.

Our guides concocted "bombs" out of corn cans and hot coals and put them on a ledge away from the camp. When those went off you certainly heard it, the boom reverberating off the canyon. We had a great meal and with then headed off to bed. Most of us were on top of the cliff about 15 feet from the water so we didn't have much of a cooling breeze that night. I tried to stay awake as long as possible to enjoy the last night on that cot under the stars. How could I ever sleep inside a building again? I remembered my first night sleeping outside on a cot, scared and nervous. Was it only 11 nights ago? It seemed like a lifetime.

Chapter 29

The Healing Power of Travelling, And How to Travel Alone

Another thing that led to my recovery and happiness is traveling, which allows you to see the world from a different perspective or point of view. When you travel with friends or family, you tend to isolate yourself from the people who live in the places you are visiting. Alone, you have no such luxury. I find that solo travelling allows you to grow as a person and discover things about yourself you never knew. So how do you travel alone, especially being female?

You can start by finding tour groups that accept singles on trips. This is easier than you would think and I do it often. I don't mean on all inclusive tours, but day tours and day trips from cities. This is a great way to meet friends, some of whom I travelled with on other trips and had dinner with. You will be able to interact with people from all continents and countries and experience different cultures and unique perspectives.

Ask friends for recommendations. What countries did they like, hotels, trips, tours?

Stay in hostels. Hostels have common areas and that is a great place to meet like-minded single travelers and you might meet someone to go exploring with.

Lonely Planet and Trip Advisor have wonderful reports and suggestions for singles and travelers. I have found their reviews spot on and useful when booking hotels.

Find an educational travel opportunity. I once studied Spanish in Guatemala which was all inclusive, including a family to stay with. This took all the stress out of bookings and I learned Spanish to boot. It was $149 a week all-inclusive including four hours of Spanish school a day.

Read nonfiction books about the country you are going to. This will familiarize you with the country and this will build excitement for the trip.

Learn some of the language of the country you are going to travel to. This is not as hard as you would think. I learned about six verbs in Spanish and how to conjugate them and about twenty nouns along with a few key phrases. That will get you through a lot of things. I also carry a translation dictionary. Carry a business card from the hotel where you are staying to give a cab driver if communication becomes too difficult.

Leave your American expectations at home. If you plan on travelling abroad, you will have a much better time if you don't constantly compare the place you are visiting to your home. If you aren't comfortable doing this, then travel in the states only. Differences are what make travel such a wonderful experience.

Study the customs of the place you are visiting. For instance, in many Latin American countries, pedestrians never have the right of way. This is important if you plan to walk around. Things like personal space, otherwise known as a bubble, varies from country to country. Don't be offended if someone is a bit too close for comfort in buses, greetings, and public places. Find out about these customs out before you travel. Knowing about where you are going and also what climate to expect will make for a much better vacation and travel experience.

Domestic travel is wonderful as well. The US is full of national and state parks to visit and explore. You can pack a tent and stay in our beautiful parks for virtually nothing.

Get a friend network of like-minded travelling folks, both single and couples. One of our trips was when ten of us rented a beach house in Roatan, Honduras, for a week. Not one person knew everyone on that trip, but we were all good friends by the end. We spent the week swimming with dolphins, learning to scuba dive, snorkeling, and just plain old fun shenanigans. Now I have more people I can turn to when the travelling bug strikes me.

Just do it. Travelling is good for the soul.

One of my greatest adventures was living with a family in Guatemala. I found a Spanish school that gave lessons and provided room and board with a host family for only $150 a week all-inclusive. I did convince a friend, Andrea, and her mother to come, but we requested separate houses so we would be forced to speak more Spanish. On the bus from Guatemala City to San Pedro la Laguna, Andrea asked me where I found this school. "Google and Trip Advisor" was my answer. I think she thought I had done a bit more research than that. Hey, they had five stars on Trip Advisor so what more could you want? We expected some sort of welcome at the school, directions, something. Instead, the van stopped at a house and the driver announced, "Adios, Maria." And I saw my family waiting for me. I almost panicked. Andrea said when they dropped me off I clung to the door with a look of terror in my eyes. It wasn't easy seeing them drive off as the family welcomed me into their home. I was out of my comfort zone. There was no English here. I met the family, saw my room, and found the toilet on the roof in an outhouse type of room and the shower off the kitchen. Then I had the most wonderful dinner with some truly spectacular people. Maria and Miguel had been hosting students for 18 years. Their three daughters had grown up with strangers from all around the world. I felt like family living with them. Only one eight-year-old daughter remained and for a week I had a little sister. I ate meals with them, shared family time at night, and saw how someone in a third world country lives. I watched Maria do more work in a day than most women in the states do in a week. No clothes washer here, you washed clothes by hand on a board. She made her own clothes and graciously made a skirt for me. She had very little in the way of modern conveniences and went to the market three times a day to make sure the food was fresh. I am not sure I have ever tasted food so good. Meat was a rarity, so most meals were vegetarian and I left feeling full and satisfied. Conversing in Spanish over meals became routine for me. As the week progressed we talked politics, health care, education, so many things. Their lives were rich in so many ways, something you just don't see from a tour bus or TV station. I feel I have another family in Guatemala. I also learned another lesson from living with them. By our standards these people were poor living in a third world country. Yet they found happiness and pleasure in the simple things. Their daughters' accomplishments, Angelina's laughter and using a small whiteboard to tell us stories at night, the taste of fresh cooked food, or eating meals with total strangers from other countries who don't speak their language. I never once failed to see Maria smile or stop what she was doing to enjoy time with her daughter and family no matter how busy she was. Things like hot water and a modern kitchen weren't important to them. They took joy from each other and the simple things. Once again I was realizing its people who make you happy, not possessions.

My friends and I did want to see some of the area and our preferred method of transport was a Tuk Tuk, a three wheeled motor vehicle that might fit three small Guatemalans, but not three Americans. Still we always crammed in one. Perhaps the highlight of our trip was in San Juan la Laguna, the next town over, and the tuk-tuk driver Arturo. Arturo saw us trying to get into a restaurant that was closed. He told us the owners were friends of his and he would call. When it was determined the restaurant was closed, Arturo offered to show us his beloved town. We went to a widows' weaving cooperative, where we had a talk on how to make things from cloth and how they still dyed everything naturally. They loved sharing with us and we walked out with many of handmade items. Next was a coffee plantation. We left our things with Arturo and went for a 5 KM hike through the plantation with a man who clearly loved his work. Arturo was waiting for us and took us to an art coop and then to his favorite restaurant for dinner with a breathtaking view of the lake. By this time Arturo was practically family. He had dinner with us, pizza and beer, and showed us pictures of his new son and his soccer trophy. The love he had for his family and city was wonderful to see. On the way back he took us to a religious processional that happens only once a year for the last 100 years or so. People lined the streets walking, singing, blowing things up, and lots of fireworks, it was an incredible sight.

Arturo found our homes, one by one, even though there are no addresses in that city, and refused to name a price for such a wonderful day. We probably gave him more than was needed and Andrea's mom gave him an extra 100 Quetzales (about $15). I hope we made his day as special as he made ours. The locals make the trip so don't isolate yourself from them. From the bread lady that talked to us every day (and stuck her head in the window when we were leaving to say bye and safe travels), to Marta who sold us some clothes and told Andrea's mother she was her mother too, to the guy herding goats up my street every morning when I walked to school and said "Good Morning" in English, to my Spanish instructor who told me about his life and taught me preterit tense, and the Guatemalan who sat next to me on the water taxi and exchanged laughter over the drunk American at the front of the boat. Some things are just funny in any language and culture. These people made me truly experience Guatemalan culture and lifestyle and made the trip so much more worthwhile. I remember being so scared when I was dropped off at the house. What an unforgettable, life changing experience I had in a country that most Americans consider third world, poor, and unsafe. Countries are made of people like us, trying to live their lives, enjoy their families, and find happiness in life.

I have been to Ecuador three times and, along with Angel, have friends there who Facebook me frequently. It makes my day to see the Facebook message pop up, "Hola, Mary, Como Estas?" from the other side of the world. I enjoy my chats with my friends from so far away. Perhaps one of my favorite people in Ecuador is Doña Cleo, who owns the restaurant where we ate at in Borja, Ecuador. Normally when we are there in kayak groups, Juliet and Ken handle the order, but I went in there two days between trips and I found what a remarkably wonderful person she is. She talks to us in Spanish and sometimes Quechua and is a shaman of considerably note. All I know is if I have stomach issues or am not feeling well, her teas will make me feel better quickly. I love listening to her stories and hearing about her cultures. She is just one more person that makes Ecuador, a place where people live, not just a spot on a map.

Joel's mother, Katy, has become almost like a sister to me. Whenever I go to Ecuador I can't wait to see her face at the Ecolodge. She has shown me how to cook popcorn without a microwave, we have cooked incredible dinners together between trips, and spent countless hours working on our Spanish and English. I feel part of her family there.

Once on a side trip to Cuenca, Ecuador, I found a fellow traveler from Houston and had a few dinners with him. We went on two tours together and I also met people from Europe and North America as we explored. My favorite thing to do is grab a city map, find some spots I want to see, and head out. Once I was reading my map trying to get a sense of direction, which is difficult since many Latin American cities don't mark their streets, when a lovely lady came up to me and asked first in Spanish if I needed help. I told her what I was looking for in Spanish and she switched to English. Her family was from Columbia, visiting as well. She could not believe I was travelling alone. My Spanish was not as good as I thought apparently. I sat with her and her family for about 30 minutes having coffee and drinks and talking about my home and hers. Just another random encounter that added to the trip. When you grab a map and wander you find yourself in unexpected places, the small art store with the artist showing his craft, the man pretending to be a statue that moves when you put money in his hat, musicians playing, children that come up and ask where you are from and ask for some English words, impromptu Spanish lessons from people trying to help, and parks and sights that just aren't always listed in Lonely Planet.

I had gotten to Cuenca by flying on an Ecuadorian Airline, another unique experience. I had only been on the International side of Quito Airport. Flying out of domestic with local Ecuadorians was quite different. First of all everything was in Spanish which was a bit of a shock, although I'm not sure why. I found myself heading out my "gate" which was really just a door in the airport that led to the tarmac with a bunch of planes. I kept taking deep breaths to quell the fear that I might get on the wrong plane. After asking numerous people and having the attendant check my ticket, I learned I was indeed on the correct plane. The airport in Cuenca was small to say the least. It took me less than fifteen minutes to get out to the taxicab and on my way for a new adventure. I had two day trips planned in Cuenca, the first was to Incipirca, an Incan city. As I walked on the Incan Road I could almost feel the presence of the Incans who had walked this road before me, I looked to the south and realized if I started walking I would end up at Machu Picchu. I was in awe that people who were considered non industrial and primitive by our modern standards could build such wonderful things that still exist so many years later. Once again I saw the world in a new light as I imagined the life that was once lived here. Their sprits live on with those of us who visit, and you can see them in the faces of the locals who are descended from them.

The second trip was quite the experience, Cajas National Park. Cajas means cold in an indigenous language. Whenever I tell people I have visited Ecuador their first reaction is it has to be hot. Actually due to the elevation Ecuador is also called the land of eternal spring. The climate is cool and wonderful in most parts. Cuenca might just have the best climate on the planet. Cajas, however, sat at elevations between 12,000 feet and 16,000 feet. We went up, up, up in our van with people from all over Europe and North America. We spent the ride learning about each other and where we lived.

We arrived at Cajas and took a beautiful flat hike around a lake and through unique vegetation at about 12,000 feet. While it was strenuous for this Florida girl, it wasn't as bad as I thought. I truly enjoyed myself. Then as we boarded the bus I realized I was mistaken, this was the warm up walk. The real hike was at 15,000 feet through a landscape that clearly looked like we were on some other planet. I was overwhelmed by the beauty of it. As I stood by the side of a cascading waterfall, taking in the scenery, I once again was filled with unbelievable happiness and fulfillment. How can any place possibly be this beautiful? The hike intensified and it started to rain. As I hiked through this crazy, amazing landscape in rain and cold, I couldn't help keep from smiling. How many people get to do this? How many people live their lives without ever taking a chance on a trip of a lifetime, an insane adventure? I was south of the equator at 15000 feet in pouring rain, freezing. It was incredible. Sure it was challenging and hard, but I saw something that many people never get to see and it was an experience of a lifetime. When we got to the end of the hike, I felt like I had accomplished something I never dreamed I could do. I hiked in extreme conditions at 15,000 feet, south of the equator, in the rain and the cold and had the time of my life! I was on top of the world, literally.

Although I hate shopping in the states, I find myself wandering through stores in big cities. In the open markets and small tiendas you can often haggle over the prices, which is something I enjoy. For food, I often find a spot filled with locals and head on in. If the menu gets too challenging you can ask for recommendations or go with the fallback of pollo con arroz , which is on every menu I have ever seen. You learn that in most Latin American countries, French fries are a vegetable and it is perfectly acceptable to have them and rice on the same plate. Fresh vegetables are truly fresh. I have never gotten sick eating in a foreign country. I don't get ice in my drinks, eat lettuce or uncooked foods, but other than that I dig right in. Often when I am eating alone, people from neighboring tables will start to talk to me, ask where I am from, what I am doing in their country and what is the US is like. I still am intimidated speaking my broken Spanish, but I have never found anyone who cares if I use the wrong word or don't roll my r's quite right. They enjoy the attempt to learn their language and most try to learn some of mine.

The first steps to travelling alone are to check out the safety of each country. For instance, Guatemala City is not safe, but the places we visited were. Large cities in general are not as safe as small ones, but I live near Atlanta, so safe is a relative thing. You wouldn't walk through a major US city in the dark carrying a camera and big purse now would you? Common sense applies when travelling as well. Pick a country that is easy to travel in for your first visit. Costa Rica is very tourist friendly, English is common, and you can even drink the tap water. Get your feet wet, traveling in a country like that first is a great idea.

I do often get help with arrangements to travel in Ecuador from Angel. On one of my Ecuador visits after Cuenca, it was suggested to me by Ken and Juliet to visit Cuyabeno. It sounded perfect, right where Columbia, Peru, and Ecuador meet. I would fly to Lago Agrio, take a bus two hours into the Amazon, board a motorized dug-out canoe, and go two more hours. Now this was way out there. I knew there was no power or running water, but I was not expecting it to be as primitive as it was. There were bunk type houses with walls and a roof way above so everything was open to the critters, no screens or glass on windows, just some mosquito netting. I literally was so terrified I was crying. I was stuck here for four days and pretty sure I was going to kill my friends when I got back to civilization. There are some serious critters in the jungle. The island we were on had a series of planks that connected our huts to the main eating hut, and a huge 75 foot tall observation tower. When they announced we were going to the lagoon I was still shaking, but the nice Australian lady in the next hut convinced me to go. It took me only ten minutes on that ride to convince me I would love the place. We saw pink river dolphins leaping in the water, monkeys in the trees, more birds than I even knew existed, and tons of wildlife. Then we jumped off the canoe and swam in the river watching the sunset over the jungle. I was in the middle of a lagoon swimming in the Amazon, watching the most beautiful sunset I've ever seen, listening to the jungle sounds, with pink diver dolphins jumping around us. I felt so lucky to be there. Then we went caiman and anaconda hunting (camera, not shooting) until it was dark and as the canoe raced back we saw flocks of bats dancing around us hunting for insects.

After an incredible meal, it was off to bed, no showers here, that was the lagoon swim. I very, very carefully tucked my mosquito netting in (although there are no mosquitoes there, something about the water does not allow them to breed), but there were tarantulas and plenty of other critters. I fell asleep listening to the sounds of the jungle. I learned some things about myself there. You really don't need as much as you think you do. Getting along with headlamps is just perfectly fine. You don't always need to lock your doors and they didn't have any locks as far as I could tell. A 12 inch frog or huge tarantula in your room can be quite fun when five guys from five different countries storm your room to get them out and have quite the heroic chase. It was the most wonderful place I have ever stayed. At 6:30 the sun comes up and every animal starts singing good morning. I crawled up the steps to the top of the tower and was in the middle of a jungle watching monkeys jump from tree to tree and more varieties of birds than you can imagine flying around. It reminded me of paradise.

The highlight of the trip was the piranha fishing. Very close to our swimming place, we set the canoes in the shallows and our guide put hunks of cow meat on a hook on a cane pole; then we churned the water with the pole and boy did they hit. Most had a piranha on their hook quickly. A lady a few rows behind me got a bit excited and her piranha went off her hook and right by my ear, I could hear its teeth clicking as it landed by my feet. The German next to me and I had our feet up on the gunnels very quickly as this very pissed off piranha thrashed around at our feet. We both had one on our own hooks not looking too happy either. Whenever anyone asks me to say one unique thing about me, I always say, "I had a live piranha thrown at me," Not too many people can say that.

The trip also included a village tour. We marched into the jungle and used machetes to cut yucca roots up. Next we went to a hut and ground the yucca to flour and drained it. After that we used the yucca flour to make yucca bread on a pan over a fire pit. I threw caution to the wind as I ate that yucca bread cooked in a very unsanitary situation without hand washing. It didn't kill me and I had a wonderful treat. Visiting a Shaman was a unique experience. The native people visit the shaman as we would a medical doctor. He told us his beliefs, shared his medicinal plants and performed a blessing/cleansing on a member of the trip. It is interesting that in modern times, many people still use shamans for medical care.

Although after drinking some of Doña Cleo's magic teas, I would visit her if she practiced in the states.

Last stop was a nature hike through the jungle. The canoe dropped us off on an island and off we went. We tasted malaria medicine from sap out of a plant and tried another sap that works as Milk of Magnesia. We learned about medicinal uses of plants, saw frogs and heard animals, and in a deluge that can only be found in a rain forest, hiked through the pouring rain in slickers across this entire island. About four hours later we emerged on the other side, wet, tired, and utterly amazed by the sights we saw.

Cuyabeno is a truly unique place. Travelling alone, I had to meet friends from many different countries. We often sat up at night looking at pictures on my IPAD and discussing the day's adventures. That Ipad survived the canoe trip in a dry bag, crazy humidity, and went all four days on a single charge, which is hard to believe it. I thought nothing could top Cajas. So in just seven days, I had lived in the Amazon and swam with Pink River dolphins, sped through a dark river watching bats swoop by, saw anacondas hang from trees, and visited an indigenous village while hiking through the rainforest. This was following the amazing Cuenca, Ingipirca, and Cajas adventures. How can anyone have this much adventure and fun in just seven short days? I had done it alone. Not bad for someone who just four years early couldn't even go to the grocery store alone or walk in the woods without getting afraid. I felt like I was healing.

So why is travelling alone so healing? In my case I felt a tremendous sense of empowerment. I could plan an international trip, book the tickets, make reservations, fly there, clear customs, and head out on my own and have a blast. I had gone from not even going to the store alone to solo international travelling. This did wonders for my self-confidence. When you feel better about yourself, your emotions will also be more positive. Sometimes I am frightened when I go off alone and I have to work through it, but I have never regretted any of my journeys or had a negative experience. In fact, the opposite is true. I always grow as a person and can't believe what a wonderful time I have on my trips.

Also when you travel alone you meet people from all walks of life. When I look back on my travels abroad and in the US, they were greatly enhanced by the people I spoke with, the clerk at the hotels, the cab drivers who are the best tour guides ever, the children on the rivers that swim with our kayaks and talk to us, and all the people that helped me with my Spanish. You see people who have less money and things then you do and yet are happier because they have family. Then you realize it isn't the material goods that make life good, it's the people. I appreciate what I have and the people who make my life good.

Chapter 30

Day 12: Miles 246 to Pearce Ferry
Mile 279.5

"You have brains in your head. You have feet in your shoes. You can steer yourself any direction you choose. You're on your own. And you know what you know. And YOU are the one who'll decide where to go..."
— Dr. Seuss, *Oh, The Places You'll Go!*

I slept straight through till around 5:15 just as the first rays of the sun were starting to make the sky less dark. I unfortunately discovered I needed to use the groover. So up I went carefully walking by my sleeping fellow adventures up into the "woods" right by where we put the snake.

When I was finished, I realized almost with regret that this is the last time I would do my business outside in that awful groover. I realized I would miss it. How odd is that? I was at first convinced I would have to hold it for 12 days and now sitting on the pot outside fairly exposed seemed as natural as breathing. As I was walking out, I saw movement by one of the cots. To my intense joy there was a kangaroo mouse hopping among everyone's belongings. I saw that Andrea was awake and whispered, "Look it's a kangaroo mouse," and all five people sleeping in that vicinity were sitting up in a heartbeat watching this mouse hopping from bag to bag hiding under things. I can't believe I got to see one! It was hopping around with its long tail behind it. You know you are with your type people, when you wake them up at 5:30 in the morning to see a mouse, and they are really excited to see it. Never be too tired to get up and experience nature.

I was not looking forward to the raft trip, seeing all the kayaks tied on and the long, long run in the hot sun. We all found a spot on one of the two rafts and off we went. It was hot, as you would expect. I somehow always managed to be on the second raft guided by Dom, otherwise known as "the great shade hunter." If there is a scrap of shade anywhere, he could find it. We spent the last day reading, enjoying the sights, and contemplating our trip

At mile 265.5 you can see the Hualapai Skywalk sticking out over one of the side canyons, otherwise known as the great toilet bowl in the sky. From the bottom looking up, you would swear you were looking into a toilet bowl. As we pulled off to an island to relieve ourselves, I wondered how many people up there with binoculars were looking down on us all peeing on the island.

And just like that the canyon ended; the sheer cliffs and spectacular views we had become accustomed to were now a memory. The frequent helicopters flying overhead were a jarring entry back to civilization.

We saw Pearce Ferry and I felt my soul drop at the thought of this perfect vacation coming to an end. We got off the rafts into the scorching heat and ate our last lunch, said good bye to the Hatch people, and piled into two vans headed to Las Vegas. I thought the air conditioner would be a welcome relief but instead it signified an end to me. Most of us slept the entire way back to Vegas. We stopped by the airport for those people leaving immediately, and the rest of us headed to South Point Casino for showers and dinner. I am not sure if culture shock describes the feeling we had in front of that casino. We stood there caked with sand, and loaded kayaks onto the cars that would transport them back, ignoring the stares of well-dressed and clean casino goers. After loading the kayaks, we agreed to meet at 6 for dinner. Most of us were leaving around midnight so Tom, Lola, Carli, and I got a room till then just for the shower. Carli and I grabbed the key and went to the gift shop to buy shampoo, conditioner, and soap. Carli got the shower first and I could hear her sounds of delight from there. When it was my turn, I was not surprised to find out the water coming off me was as brown as the Colorado River. Where was it all coming from? I washed my hair three times and dirt was still pouring out. I don't think a shower has ever felt so good. By the time the four of us were done shower, the tub was clogged and very dirty, but clean we were.

We had dinner in a prime rib restaurant, super fancy with many courses and real butter in the shape of flowers. I still could not believe how good cold water tasted. We enjoyed each other's company for one last time with new and old friends and then headed up to get our gear and head to the airport.

I was feeling pretty good about things in general, although I was not happy to leave and ready to leave at the same time. I couldn't imagine not seeing the spectacular sights I was seeing on a daily basis, but I have to admit I had enjoyed that shower and clean clothes. I had been told that this place would change me, which it was a spiritual place, and it was. I'm not sure if it was the environment, people, or lack of electronics and modern comforts. But I had come to terms with a lot of things on this trip that needed to be dealt with. I knew I still had a way to go, but journeying down that canyon was a mirror to my life journey, full of bends, bumps, challenges, beauty, fun, discovery, and friends. But I find it hard to believe that anyone can go down that canyon like we did and not be changed for the good forever. One thing is for certain a part of me will always be in the canyon and longing to return.

Chapter 31

Final Musings

It has been a long eight years since Jim passed and started my life on such an emotional journey. I never imagined where I would end up after sitting with Jim's body wondering how I could ever get along. There is a country song by George Straight called *She Let Herself Go* that my friend says is my theme song. I have gone from an insecure, scared woman who couldn't sleep alone in a house without all the lights on or go to the store alone to someone who travels alone internationally, can speak in Spanish somewhat, kayaks, backpacks, hikes alone, and is becoming the person I want to be, confident, secure, and most of all happy. I still have days when I hear Jim's voice telling me I am not good enough or smart enough to do something or face insecurities dealing with people with confidence, but those voices are lower and lower and less and less as the years go by. I feel that the person I was eight years ago has been reborn into someone new, a rebirth so to speak.

I notice how little things rarely upset me. Once on the way to a river on a two-lane mountain road, we found ourselves stopped by emergency vehicles and a helicopter. Instead of being upset by the delay, I gave thanks I wasn't the poor guy having to be airlifted out. I enjoyed the sunshine, crisp air, and beautiful scenery. If someone wants to cut me in line, go right ahead. I rarely speed when driving any more. I try to enjoy the scenery. If I see some cool overlook or view I will stop and enjoy it. If you are always in a rush to get to specific destinations, then you might miss something spectacular and uplifting as you speed by. I always try to leave some time on my driving trips to stop in case I see something interesting to visit.

I have always loved to talk, but now I really enjoy talking to just about everyone and am surprised by how enjoyable it is to talk to strangers about experiences they have had or just sharing the view. I must admit that I have been late to rivers or events because I have had the pleasure of talking to people at rest stops, scenic views, or other impromptu stops. I smile more and give greetings to people more frequently, which I noticed people do in Latin America. I like it and it makes the day more pleasant. But on the flip side, it is also important to be comfortable being alone with yourself. I cherish the times I have in my house now alone without anyone dictating my life. I have learned to enjoy my own company.

I also think I am a better teacher, a better listener. Kids I don't even teach often come to me to talk and for advice. I think they know I genuinely care about them and although I have no counselor training, I have experienced a lot of grief and trying times, and those kids know that and know I can understand what they are so desperately trying to come to terms with. Sometimes just having a sympathetic ear is all you really need. I have been there and I do care and understand. Middle school kids have so many issues to deal with, and I will always listen to them. Teaching is more than just academics and state mandated high stakes testing. I will never be so hurried to get through the curriculum or to practice for a state test that I won't listen to a student tell me she is worried because her beloved little brother is in the hospital sick or someone has called her a name and she can't cope. Some things are just too important to rush through. People are what are most important.

It is also extremely important to remember that other people have gone through what you have gone through. I know it seems impossible to believe when you are wracked with grief that anyone could possibly relate to your grief, but I guarantee you someone has experienced it. Whenever I am talking to someone who needs a shoulder to cry on and I tell them I lost a husband, two sisters, a brother in law, a newborn niece, my mom, and a friend in a few years, they can only stare in shock. But surely they have lost someone and can relate. Grief and dealing with death is something that all human beings have in common. And in mutual compassion you will find healing.

Take a chance, talk to someone. There is a tremendous feeling of relief when you feel that connection with someone who has experienced the same type of trauma. Sometimes when you just talk to them you can feel the tension in your shoulders, and I am not sure if I can put into words the overall relief you feel when you realize that someone understands you. We had two teachers lose husbands in consecutive years after mine. I felt like we were some part of a club that no one wants to actually be in. We comforted each other in a way no one else could. There is comfort in mutual suffering and understanding.

Something I did that unexpectedly made a huge difference in my life, happiness, and healing was to get rid of the TV. I still have one for the occasional movie, but without the burden of having the TV, I actually have to go out and live. I take walks, practice my Spanish, visit with people, or read a book. TV can be a trap; you can't find true happiness staring at a TV watching other people live their lives. It can prevent you from living. Don't believe me? Try this, just for one week, no TV. See how much your life will improve. Now take the $100 a month you will save and you can travel to some wonderful vacation once a year with that money and really live and enjoy life.

Counseling and therapy are also imperative for most people to adequately recover. They are trained to help and can help you deal with your emotions. Why isolate yourself and not avail yourself of every opportunity to get better and be happy? You have to make a choice to help yourself and take every opportunity to do so. I often still sign up for a few counseling lessons. I've never once regretted that.

Growth and enlightenment can come from tragedy if you let it. While none of my experiences were pleasant and I wish I hadn't experienced them, I learned from them and grew. I'm a better person. Holding the hands of loved ones in their final moments is the most gut-wrenching thing you can deal with, but I still take pleasure in the fact that I was with them to the end and they felt my love. I relish the loved ones I have remaining. I know how important family is. Playing Yahtzee with my sister, seeing my brother make stained glass creations, and watching my nieces and nephews grow up and start families fill me with joy. My cousins are far spread and numerous and through Facebook I have managed to contact some of them and am part of their lives as well.

Follow your dreams. I completed my doctorate degree in 2012. I wish my parents could have lived to see it. Both had wanted to attend college and were unable to. My love of education and continuing it is due to the values they instilled on me. I have always wanted to teach college, and I kept applying for many openings until I finally landed a part time online job at Post University, a private college in Connecticut. I am hoping this will lead to full time online employment so I can travel more. Just because a goal is hard to reach doesn't make it impossible. Everyone said you need experience to land a college job, but I kept applying anyway. The only true obstacle you have is yourself. Tell yourself it is possible; then keep trying till you succeed.

Get your bucket lists trips and do them. Wow, I still can't believe I paddled and rafted 280 miles of the Grand Canyon. The experiences there changed me forever, and I still long to be back there sleeping by the river and under the stars. There are certain places on earth that have a healing effect, almost spiritual. Find that place for you and go spend time there away from technology and everyday life stresses.

Sometimes things happen to us that are so terrible, so life altering, so unbelievably awful, that we see no way to live through them. I have learned that good things sometimes come from bad things. I now appreciate things more and I rarely get very angry or upset. I am happier than I have been since my childhood. These bad events have shaped me into the person I have become. I wish my sisters, mother, father, and brother-in-law could still be here, but I have their memories and I live each day to the fullest and remember all the happy times I had with them. In the end, how you deal with things and what you learn from them are more important than the events themselves. We can't live in a world without loss or unhappy things happening. But we can take strength in the knowledge that we can emerge from the tragedy enlightened and thankful for what we have. I often tell my students that everything in life is a choice and how you respond to adversity is a choice. I choose to be happy and find pleasure in life. Life is an adventure, and everyone should enjoy it to the fullest. Find your own happiness in the world and never let go.

Purchase other Black Rose Writing titles at

www.blackrosewriting.com/books

and use promo code PRINT to receive a 20% discount.

CPSIA information can be obtained at www.ICGtesting.com
Printed in the USA
LVOW11s0759150415

434671LV00002B/4/P